Sorting Through the Past

Sorting
Through
the Past

Sorting Through the Past

by Linda Hilton

To Scott and Megan, with love

Contents

Sorting room by room   32

Chapter 3   73

Chapter 4   81

Preface

Over the years I have been faced with the daunting task of sorting through possessions after someone has died – not the most exciting of prospects, but something all of us have to deal with sooner or later in life.

In one case several of us had months on end to deal with a house full of furniture, clothes, dishes and family treasures. We lived in town, and there was no hurry to empty or sell the house. On another occasion two of us were faced with completely clearing out a small one bedroom house and garage, selling a car, closing out bank accounts and holding a funeral all in three days, and that included travel time from another state and back.

In between I have flown across the country alone and faced sorting through belongings of two generations and six people's stuff in one home, deciding in a week what to ship home and what to leave behind, what to give away and what to throw away.

I have helped old childhood friends who have a week in the town where we grew up and I still live, sort through 40 years of clutter and pack up a lifetime of memories. In some cases the amount of goods pack-ratted away is overwhelming, if not astounding. For others, even through the person possessed very little at first glance, there was a seemingly unending amount of things to be dealt with.

Whatever the situation, it was always stressful and overwhelming. One of the biggest challenges was where to start. There are obvious treasures to take home, obvious junk to be thrown away. But what do you do with all the rest of it?

I came to develop a system which has helped me immensely when faced with the task of sorting through cupboards in which important, vital documents have been buried between ancient recipes and extra napkins, drawers where jewelry has been thrown in with lipsticks and partial tubes of ointment, storage rooms where a christening dress is found in an old picnic basket and books are stacked to the ceiling. Then there are the boxes containing 45 years of utility bill stubs, 250 issues of National Geographic, pieces of long ago discarded appliances and a collection of ceramic dwarfs that not one family member wants to take home, much less display!

What's a person to do? Start with a plan! And if all else fails, ask for help. I am now a professional organizer who helps clients through this process each week. If you decide to seek help from a professional organizer, you can find the best by going to The National Association of Productivity and Organizing Professionals (NAPO) website, napo.net, or contacting the professional organizer's association in your state.

My hope is that this informative book will be of help when you are faced with sorting through your or someone else's past. Best wishes and much success. You CAN do this. Now let's get started!

Introduction

Whether you are cleaning out a family home after the death of a loved one, helping a friend through the process, or preparing to downsize yourself or someone else to smaller living quarters, there is something in this guide for you! There are sections on questions to ask before taking action, ideas for where to donate lots of things you'll find around the house, and a special section in Chapter 4, on how to downsize yourself or someone you love in anticipation of a move to a smaller living space.

I have found uncashed checks for thousands of dollars. I have found money and jewelry stashed in boxes of cleaning powder. One of my family members saved silver coins and ingots in makeup jars under the bathroom sink. While going through old purses of another relative, I came across over $3,000 of expired travelers checks. The money was recovered! I have found stock certificates and family photos mixed in with utility bill receipts and expired coupons. Check through everything!

This book also applies to any situation where an heir or executor is given the seemingly insurmountable task of sorting through and dispensing with everything accumulated during another person's lifetime.

Chapter 1

Key questions to ask before beginning

Who will be involved in making decisions?

From the beginning you must decide who will be involved in making decisions. If dealing with an estate, be sure to check with the family lawyer and/or the estate executor before taking anything out of the house because often the disposition of some items has been predetermined. There may be specific instructions in the will regarding who should be in charge of doing what when settling the estate.

I have found on more than one occasion that family members are prohibited from even throwing a pile of plastic containers into a recycling bucket until pictures have been taken or a representative of the attorney's office has done a full inventory of the estate and has taken pictures.

Often, for estates of those without children, a single heir has been appointed as the executor. In most cases I dealt with there are usually no other relatives left. Is there any provision in the will for the "estate" to hire help?

If there are just a few children, will the decisions be made by all? Or will spouses be included in the decision-making process? Will children, grandchildren, nieces and nephews get a say in what happens?

If there are numerous children and all are married, will the decisions be made only by the children, or will their spouses be included? Regarding spouses, it should be all or none unless some spouses are not able to participate, for whatever reason. Inclusion of grandchildren, nieces and nephews should also be discussed. If some children are married and others are not, that could throw decision making out of balance if spouses are included. The same goes for grandchildren.

Think about having one person per family serve on a family committee charged with disbursing and disposing of items left as part of the estate. Each child can serve or appoint one member of his/her immediate family to serve on the "family committee" as representative. If you elect to have a family committee, everyone in the family must agree to abide by the decisions of the committee to the end. Depending on your circumstances, you may want to put this in writing — not necessarily a legal document but one that you can go back to if tempers flare after certain decisions are made — and have everyone involved sign it.

Consider making specialized family committees or appointing certain family members to take care of particular things depending on who has certain knowledge or expertise. If you have a family member who knows a lot about insurance, put him/her in charge of all hospital and nursing home bills to sort and get straightened out. Those with good knowledge of tools and power equipment can be in charge of sorting and evaluating everything in the garage workshop. The best negotiator in the family can be put in charge of selling the car, and so forth.

I have dealt with families where everyone wants to help in some way. A good way of including all members, especially younger members, is to have them help with sorting items. In the kitchen, they can look at expiration dates on food containers and throw out items that are past their prime. In the shop, get some shoe boxes and let older kids sort general tools into them, screwdrivers in one box, hammers in another. Sort recycling, go through socks and throw away those with holes or no mates, match up plastic cups and containers with lids. These are a few ways to make everyone feel useful and are duties that adults don't need to be involved in for the short term. Older teens LOVE to drive so have them load and deliver donations to charity.

One of my clients was a semi-professional seamstress who sewed many items for family and friends. After her death, two of her granddaughters were put in charge of sorting out all of the patterns. Wedding dresses, regular clothes, curtains, decorations, baby quilts. They also organized all the material by type of fabric. This made donating items in her sewing studio so much easier as different organizations had different needs.

What is the security level at the home, condo or apartment?

There may be many keys in circulation. Do friends, neighbors, the nursing agency, or others have keys to the property? Does anyone know how many are out there? If the estate owns the property, consider changing the locks RIGHT NOW if you are going to leave items there for awhile unattended. If dealing with a rented apartment, ask the main office if the locks can be changed. Nosy neighbors or friends might have verbally been promised items and some have no second thoughts about stopping by and helping themselves to those and other items.

I was clearing an estate and came back one morning to find a lady in the home going through the kitchen cupboards. "Where is the asparagus steamer?" she asked? "Mary promised I could have it. And the rocking chair is mine, too! She promised." As we were speaking in the kitchen, unknown to me, her husband was going out the front door with the rocker. By the time I went back to the living room, the chair was long gone! Even if there is an alarm system or keypad to open the garage, it is best to assume that more than one person has the code. Change it right now. You might also want to think about having a trusted relative or friend live at the house until you get things cleared out or can come back to town and deal further with the situation. This goes a long way toward keeping thieves who monitor death and funeral notices away. One more note: if the property will be empty for awhile, make removing small valuable items like computers and jewelry a priority.

Who pays for what?

Whether you are dealing with a large or small estate, money is always a touchy issue. Even if there is plenty of money in the estate and everyone in the family seems to get along, you should still answer a few questions before dividing things up. If nothing else, you will all know "the rules" from the start, and no one will be taken by surprise when someone asks the keeper of the checkbook to write a check to UPS for shipping a set of dishes from Ohio to California, or moving a piano 100 miles away.

Often, at least one heir lives in town, and others do not. Some may live a few hours drive away while others live across the country. For those who live far away, there is the question of getting items from the family home to their present home. You will all need to decide up-front who will pay for any expenses to get items from one home to another and agree on what expenses are "fair."

You may also have different perspectives on what to do with various items throughout the house, depending on your up-front decisions and the answers to the following questions.

- Should those who paid a lot to get home for the cleaning-out project be allowed to have the estate pay for shipping costs of the items they want? Should there be a limit on this allowance?
- Should the estate pay for shipping only small packages – say dishes and books – but not for shipping rocking chairs and china cabinets? What about specialty items like a piano? Again, should there be an allowance to cover part of the costs?
- Should those within a day's drive be allowed money for renting a truck or trailer to haul furniture home? How about gas money? For those who may rent a vehicle and drive home for more than one day, will meals and motels be covered?
- Should each family or family member involved be given a moving / shipping allowance to use as they see fit regardless of where they live? It may cost as much to move a piano across town as it does to ship a few framed pictures several hundred miles.

How should sentimental items be divided and distributed?

Sentimental items are those of little value outside the family – mom's favorite afghan, dad's hand-carved walking stick, mom and dad's wedding portrait, beloved holiday decorations. Sometimes these items are the most fought over because of the memories associated with them. To help alleviate arguments and hurt feelings, here are two systems I have created: Round Robin and Family Lottery. They may ease the pain and burden. These systems can also be used to help divide up furniture and other household items in a more "fair" way.

Before deciding which method to use you must decide who will participate – spouses, children, nieces, cousins. Count the number of people participating and number of items to be divided. My rule of thumb – If there are more items than people, use Round Robin; more people than items use Family Lottery.

One last thing before dividing and distributing stuff. Check certain items around the house, both large and small, to see if the deceased put names on some or all of the items.

What is Round Robin?

Round Robin is a way to distribute items, especially those that are one-of-a-kind sentimental, in an amicable way among family members who want them. Put all the items to be distributed on a table or in the center of one room. Draw lots to see who picks first, second and third. The first person picks the item they want most, and takes it with NO discussion or controversy from the others. The second person does the same. Go around the circle until all items are taken. If they don't come out even, take the last few items and have a family lottery, described next, if you cannot agree that an uneven total will be OK. If emotions are running high, lots can be redrawn after each round or the second person starts the second round and the third person picks first in the third round. If there are a lot of items, perhaps there are twelve items and three people want them, then each person will get four.

How do you have a Family Lottery?

For just a few treasures that many family members want, put the items on a table or together in one area. Place a bowl in front of each item. Pass out slips of paper and pens to all those participating. Have those who want a particular item put their names on a slip of paper and put it in the bowl in front of that item. Everyone can fill out one piece of paper for as many items as he/she wants. Then ask someone who is not a lottery participant to draw a name out of the bowl in front of the most sought-after item. The person whose name is drawn takes the item and is eliminated from getting any other item. If that person's name is drawn for a subsequent item, the slip is ignored and another name is drawn unless one or more of the last items has only one name in the bowl. In that case, can everyone agree that the person whose name is in the bowl be given a second item?

A version of family lottery is to have everyone put their name in one bowl. The person whose name is drawn first gets to pick the item they most want. He/she is then ineligible for any other item. Continue drawing names until all items are gone. If family lottery is used more than once, consider having two separate bowls, one with the names of those who were left out of the last lottery, the other with the rest of the names.

How do we make sure everything is "fair?"

Some families have no problem dividing up most remaining items and coming to an agreement of what is more or less "fair." Often there is more to be dispersed than anyone wants to take home. But, in some families there can be a lot of contention among siblings. Someone often thinks one particular brother or sister will get the best of everything and end up with more than his/her fair share. If this is the case and avoiding all-out family war is your number-one priority, hire an appraiser and have everything of value appraised. Perhaps you will even need to have everything, down to the last bowl appraised. This will cost the estate some money but the knowledge that everyone will get exactly the same dollar amount of items as everyone else will be worth current and lasting peace. Be sure to determine if the estate or every heir or just the "complainers" will pay the expense.

After the appraisal is finished, draw lots as described in the Round Robin section and have each person pick one item at a time. Ask someone outside the family to keep track of "spending" for each family member. When you get close to the end, those with larger totals cannot pick any more items until those with small totals catch up. You might also want to consider that whoever picks first in a round sets the price for the round. For example the spending limit for round one is $200. Your sister goes first and picks an item worth $200 dollars. You are next and most want an item valued at $75. You are allowed to pick that item and $125 in other items. It is up to you what rules you set for the process, but be sure everyone understands and agrees to the rules before you start "shopping." If necessary, write down all the rules and have everyone sign that they agree to abide by them TO THE END.

Family Auction

Another idea is to have a family auction with play money. This might sound a bit silly but it does work. Have everything appraised or have a neutral party price all items you want in the auction. Then instead of everyone taking turns picking one item at a time, give everyone in the family the same amount of play money and an equal chance to get the most coveted items. Make sure there is enough play money distributed per person that bidding can go a bit over the set price of the most prized family possessions. Pick items that are most desired by the majority of family members, and ask a friend or neighbor "to auction" the items, one at a time. Start your auction with the items which the most people want. To determine these items, give each bidder, or bidding unit (family) three small self-sticking colored dots to put on the items they are most interested in bidding on.

An opening bid is usually set for half of the appraised value/price. The top bidder gets that item. Work your way down the list until every item that more than one person desires is "sold." Some family members will only get a few items and others will get more but everyone has an equal chance to get the "best" things. If one person chooses to blow everything on mom's china hutch in the first round, that is their decision. After auctioning off items that more than one person wants, continue in the Round Robin fashion, as described earlier, until everything is "sold" and everyone is out of "money," or everyone involved decides that anything that is left is to be taken by anyone who wants it. Prices paid during Round Robin are the full appraised value of every item. No negotiating, or there will almost certainly be a fight. If everyone has spent all of their play money and there are items left, decide how much more money to distribute, and continue on to round two if needed. On some occasions, one sibling may want a lot of furniture while the others want just a few dishes and some knick-knacks. If this is the case, you might want to use play money until one sibling announces that he/she is done "shopping." This is most common when one or more family members who live long distances away or in small homes, condos or apartments have all the items they have room to take or store. At that point, you may all decide that the heir who is done will be allowed to be "cashed out" by the estate. In other words, that person receives $200 extra cash from the estate while everyone else keeps shopping. This "rule" will often apply when large ticket items like cars and recreational items like boats and campers need to be sold. BE SURE this is part of the discussion before you undertake any round robin or family lottery activity.

Do you want to have a yard sale?

If time is more precious than money, don't do this! In most cities, there is a place where almost everything can be donated. Chapter 2 has guidelines and suggestions for donating most items around the house and in the garage, both ordinary and specialized, and suggestions for how to sell or disburse more valuable items no one wants to take home.

If you are thinking of or going to have a yard sale, here are some questions to ask before you begin:

- Will one person in the family be put in charge of this event?
- Will one person or family be in charge of pricing and deciding what to do with the leftovers, or will you have a family yard sale committee?
- Who will get the proceeds? Will only those family members who help with the sale get the proceeds? Or, will the proceeds go to the estate to be divided later? Should those holding the sale be paid a flat rate by the estate? This is a great job for teenagers and young adults.
- Should you put all your items out for sale? Consider how you might feel seeing strangers plowing through your mother's wardrobe and trying on her dress coat or shoes in the front yard. It may be too difficult to watch. Do you want nosy neighbors coming over to go through jewelry and hats? How will you feel if they buy those items? Consider donating more personal items to charity up front.

If you do hold a yard sale, and money is of secondary importance, you may want to donate yard sale proceeds to your loved one's favorite charity, remembering to put that information in your advertisements. That might also inspire people from the recipient group to offer help in running the sale. It certainly will help drive sales if someone is crazy about animals and sees that all proceeds will go to the local animal shelter or rescue organization. Consider letting teenaged grandchildren who are more interested in money than in family heirlooms do most of the work for the yard sale in exchange for a portion of the proceeds.

When going ahead with a yard sale, consider carefully what you will offer for sale. Is some of this stuff truly junk? There is no need to waste energy displaying, and pricing items that you will end up throwing away at the end of the day. No one will buy half bottles of perfume or partially burned candles. Rule of thumb – when in doubt, throw it out!

At the end of the sale you will be glad you did. If you absolutely cannot throw something out, like half used bottles of perfume, consider having a FREE table at the sale. Maybe you will feel better seeing the stuff taken away. Don't forget to advertise your "FREE" table.

If you are selling loads of items from a house and literally everything goes, consider putting some items out front as a draw but leaving most items in the home. Put all the drinking glasses together in a cupboard and put a sign on the door, "All glasses 50 cents". This will save you lots of time and energy setting up tables in the yard, hauling out every item, and pricing each item.

My team had an entire home to clear. Time was short, we were called in to set up a sale in five days. The deceased was a single uncle who had left everything to his only niece. Items ranged from office supplies to hand soap, furniture to clothing, to a huge room of tools. We went with the easiest solution. Throw out the obvious junk and give away personal items like underwear, then price the big stuff and leave all the little, everyday stuff in place. We put a table of the valuable items next to the cashier with everything nicely displayed and individually priced. The shoppers were told they could go through every drawer, cabinet and closet, the workroom, backyard shed and small garage. Whatever they wanted to buy they should bring to the cashier and make an offer. The cashier had final say on prices but most people offered a fair deal. The shoppers had so much fun likening the sale to a scavenger hunt. More than 90 percent of the things in the house were sold in four hours. We were able to empty the rest of the house in a couple of hours.

A word here about "collectables." The resale market across the nation for items that are sold in large quantities, generally through newspapers, direct mail, or shopping channels, is almost non-existent. I have had clients with collections of porcelain dolls, commemorative coins, annually issued

Christmas plates and the like become hysterical when told that this stuff is not worth anything. Many people considered items advertised as collectables to be items that would increase in value over time. That is usually far from the truth. The younger generations don't want these items. One client had made a huge investment in commemorative coins, thinking he would have extra money at retirement when he cashed them in only to be told by a very reputable coin dealer that the coins were only worth face value and the fancy packaging and framing was worth nothing. He lost hundreds of dollars in the end. If donating these items to charity is too heart-wrenching, put a nominal price on each item, and advertise heavily that proceeds will go to a charity favored by you or the deceased who owned the items.

I had a client who inherited over 100 dolls from her grandmother. She couldn't GIVE them away to anyone in the family. What to do? There are people out there who do collect dolls, so we devised a plan. She would offer the dolls, many of famous people, for $5 each. All proceeds would go to the local food bank — a place her grandmother gave money and food to annually. The ad headline was, "Buy a doll, feed a child." Then details about the low prices and where the proceeds were going were included. At the sale the granddaughter was able to chat about her grandmother, and almost every doll sold within the three hour sale! Everyone loved the event and it was a win-win.

Consignment stores may offer you a route to sell things that are larger – bookcases, buffets, dining table and chairs. Look online to see what stores are in your area and call or visit to see what items they might take. It is surprising what some places resell. A few local dealers in my area resell not only furniture but art, nicer dishes and glassware, and some décor pieces. After those prime items are gone, you might just want to call the charity truck to pick up the rest. If time is short but there are some really nice pieces of jewelry or other valuables, maybe even funky, items that you cannot consign in your area, consider donating them to an upcoming charity auction or sale. Every charity I am associated with has an annual fundraising event which most often has a silent auction. This is a great way to support a cause dear to the heart of your family and help a local charity get great items to sell.

I have had many clients inherit lots of jewelry that they will never wear. It is not that the pieces are low quality, it is that the pieces are not of interest to them. Perhaps the style – southwest or Victorian – is not what they wear. Perhaps they don't like pieces with green stones or blue accents. Some people prefer silver jewelry over gold, and vice versa. Whatever the reason, these pieces are prime candidates for an auction. One of my clients donated a beautiful antique Sterling silver cosmetic set, one client donated a funky retro cabinet with a hidden bar inside, yet another donated some stylized art pieces to a group with an audience for that type of art. Some clients were focused on benefiting a certain ethnic or religious group.

Should we consider an estate sale?

An estate sale is typically larger than a yard sale, has more high-end items and runs over a period of days. This is a good solution for larger homes with a wide variety of antiques, art and jewelry, and is best done by a company that specializes in estate sales and has a certified appraiser on staff. Get references, make sure the company is licensed and bonded and will provide enough staff to help customers throughout the property.

What about an auction?

Some houses are full of antiques, quality furniture for which no one has room or fancy dishes and large collections that are not of interest to anyone in the family. Families may be more interested in selling the bulk of items rather than dividing things and moving them out. If that is the case and you have decided to forego an estate sale, consider hiring an auctioneer who specializes in liquidating estates. Find out upfront if items can be sold on site or if the company requires that every item be moved to an auction house. The auctioneer can put smaller items into lots and determine starting bids on everything. A reputable auction house can also tell you what will or won't sell well at auction. This is a good way to move nicer items quickly and a good solution if you don't want the public wandering through your property. Auction companies may also liquidate estates for a fee. Some auction houses will come to your home; others require everything be moved to their facility. Fees may or may not include packing and moving everything to the auction house. Be sure to check with your local Better Business Bureau to verify the company's reputation and ask for references if you have the slightest doubt about who you are dealing with. Auctioneers can be found online, or you might also ask a trusted lawyer or accountant for a referral.

I fight an ongoing battle with clients who think their stuff is worth a lot of money because they saw it listed on eBay for a great amount. One client wanted me to sell a figurine for $100 for her. I told her it was worth $5-10. She wouldn't listen until we went on the eBay site and saw what the BIDS were on that item. Sure, there were 37 seemingly identical items listed, some as high as $150. What the client needed to pay attention to were the three items that had bids, for $5, $7 and $7.50 after being posted for over 90 days. THIS shows what the public will pay for the item and sets the true value of whatever someone has to sell.

Is recycling a priority at this point?

You need to have a frank upfront discussion about this so that someone in the family doesn't come unglued when 12 years of magazines are thrown away instead of being put in a box for recycling or taken to a recycling center. Here are some questions to ask:

- What items are going to be recycled?
  Are they items generally accepted by curbside services and recycling centers, like paper and plastic, or are they items like metal or electronics that some adamant recycler is committed to move out? For ideas of places that take more specialized items see Chapter 2.
- Is there a community curbside recycling program?
  If so, how often do they pick up and how much do they take at each pickup? If there is too much for one week, is someone in the family available and WILLING to see the project through to the end?
- Is there storage space for all that should be picked up later?
- If there is no curbside program, do those who are adamant about recycling now have time to take EVERYTHING to a recycling center? How far away is the center? What are the hours? What EXACTLY do they take? Things can change quickly depending on the recycling after-market, so call ahead.
- Are you being realistic?

Does everyone who is interested in seeing items recycled understand the amount to be disposed of? A basement closet full of newspapers becomes a larger amount than first thought once you start hauling it out of the house. If you are in doubt, take a quick inventory tour of the house, garage and any storage sheds.

Is there a proper vehicle to take recycling to a center? To pull off such a project, you won't be able to haul much in a rented sub-compact car. Making innumerable trips gets old fast, especially if the recycling center is some distance away. Consider the time factor, cost of gas, possible vehicle rental and mileage charges.

How do we dispose of a mountain of trash?

Unless your family member lived a Spartan existence, there is more to throw out in the average house than you could ever dream! Find out when garbage day is and how much trash can be put out at one time. If you are cleaning out an apartment or condominium with communal garage dumpsters, check with the manager to see how much you are allowed to put out at one time. You may be fined if you fill up one complete dumpster. If you do not have residential trash collection or if you are cleaning out a large or very cluttered property, consider renting a dumpster or hiring someone with a large truck to haul things to the dump. You may want to use some funds from the estate for this expense. It is money well spent, and I highly recommend it.

In larger cities and suburban areas, inquire with the city or county sanitation department, listed on line, about dumpster rental programs. You can also find dumpsters for rent by looking through on-line classified ads sponsored by your local media. This is often cheaper than going with bigger national companies.

If your community does not have dumpster service, you have several options. Ask a neighbor, or look in the local classifieds for someone with a truck that you can hire to take things to the dump. If the deceased was a member of a local faith community or supported a local nonprofit organization with time and/or money, call and ask if someone in the organization is willing to hire out for this or volunteer to do this in exchange for a donation to the charity.

Franchises of 1-800-GOT-JUNK? are springing up around the country. Call or look online to see if your zip code is served. Booking a pick-up online will save you money. This is a great service, and they clean up after the junk is removed; every scrap of paper is gone and every bit of dirt is swept up. Prices are set by how much volume your stuff takes up in their truck.

What do I do with everything else?

Call and get lists from local charitable organizations, especially those that the deceased supported financially or where he/she spent time volunteering. Ask about pickup service; it is not always available. If there is no pickup service, explain your situation and time table. Ask the organization if they have a volunteer who was a good friend of the deceased who would be willing to come pick up some items.

Now it's time to get down to work and start wading through closets, cupboards, drawers and boxes of seemingly endless stuff. Chapter 2 has suggestions for ways to get started and how to get most household items to places that can use them. For suggestions on how to deal with all the photographs, see Chapter 2. Help for sorting all those papers, paperwork and documents can be found in Chapter 3. These are ideas that anyone can use right now even if downsizing is a few years away or you are just tired of piles and boxes taking up space in your home.

Whether you are downsizing or dealing with an estate, this is a stressful, emotional time for all involved. It is vital to keep clear communication flowing among all those involved in bringing the situation to a conclusion. Remember to take care of yourself and others involved by taking plenty of breaks, eating well, and staying hydrated. Listen to uplifting music. Take time to share memories that certain items bring back. Take the opportunity to vent and tell others how silly or ugly you think something is. You may all have a good laugh together.

Do the best you can and strive to be kind to one another.

Chapter 2

Getting Started

Items you will need to assemble before starting your sorting process include:

- Sturdy boxes – free from some local businesses or you can buy boxes at home improvement stores like Home Depot and Lowes, shipping and packing stores or your local U-Haul dealer who gives you the option of ordering boxes online and having them delivered!
- Garbage bags – lots of big, sturdy ones – not just for garbage! Try to get black, green, white and clear. More about this later.
- Packing tape – for assembling boxes, or sealing those that you will ship or drive home.
- Scotch tape
- Sticky notes and pens
- Some larger sheets of paper or poster board and a marker
- Old newspapers or packing paper to wrap things in
- Rags for dusting and cleaning
- Paper towels
- Ziploc bags, several sizes
- Bubble wrap or packing peanuts
- Computer, if possible; you might want to bring your own laptop.
- Digital camera, optional but helpful in some cases

Now you are ready to tackle the process

No matter the type of item, whether you are dealing with items in one cupboard or an entire room, EVERYTHING can be rough-sorted into three major categories —

Keep, Give, Throw

You may decide to add a fourth category — Recycle! Or a fifth — Consign and Sell. This will become your mantra. Make three or four big signs with the words KEEP, GIVE, and THROW or write these words in large letters on three good sized boxes. This may seem silly now, but after your third hour sorting through closets, you will lose track of which pile or box is which and nothing is worse than discovering that for the last hour you have been putting KEEP and THROW items in the same box. If you have decided to hold a yard sale or use a consignment store, you will want to add one more box that says SELL. In the beginning, put all MAYBES in the KEEP box. These include items another family member may want but you don't. More about that later. Put a large CLEAR trash bag in the GIVE box. When it is full take it to a pre-designated area of the house for future action. Put a large BLACK trash bag in the THROW box. If you have recycling, put a large GREEN trash bag in that box, and WHITE trash bags can go in the SELL box. Using a color-coded bag system helps keep donation and trash separated and is a huge help when you are halfway to the garage with a bag, get interrupted and then try to remember later what was in the bag. The color will remind you where it goes.

Start with one room. I recommend something small, easy and more emotionally neutral like the bathroom or laundry room, as opposed to the more daunting kitchen or emotionally charged memorabilia storage area. Designate a space where you will put your KEEP, GIVE, and THROW boxes. If you are in doubt as to where an item should go in KEEP or GIVE, put it in KEEP and revisit it later being VERY careful not to use this as a fallback. If a particular drawer or cupboard becomes too overwhelming, skip it and come back later. Do the best you can. This is not an easy job!

When sorting it is also best to follow this basic guideline – When in doubt, throw it out! Don't even consider donating or trying to sell any item that is broken, has missing pieces, or is in disrepair. This includes clothing covered in pet hair, missing buttons, stained. These should be disposed of! Charities do NOT have time to make repairs. Again,

When it doubt, throw it out!

Many items can be used by local nonprofit and some governmental agencies if you have a long period of time to sort and deliver or come across items that are more challenging to find a new home for. See specific recommendations later in this chapter. There, listed in alphabetical order, are items that many of you will have to deal with. If you have problems finding a certain item, check the index in the back of this book for a more detailed list. Headings that follow are broad. Many items have been grouped for simplicity.

There are many suggestions for making donations to nonprofit organizations that serve specific populations such as seniors or people with disabilities. For help in finding these organizations I strongly recommend utilizing 2-1-1. This phone number has been set aside nationwide for referrals to local nonprofit agencies for services, volunteers and donations, sort of a 4-1-1- for social services. Currently the phone number operates in all 50 states, but check www.211.org to find out if your area is covered.

The best thing on the web for finding a home for almost anything — and I mean anything — on the planet is **freecycle.org**. You can offer the strangest items – half a bag of cement mix, 17 bricks, even things that need repair. There are chapters not only across the U.S. but in other countries as well. Local chapters are formed and moderated by volunteers. If there is not a chapter in your area start one using instructions on the website. Membership is free but you must sign up with the group in your area and follow simple, no-brainer rules to post items you offer. One caution, once you sign on, your email will be bombarded with items wanted, offered and taken. There is always the unsubscribe button if it gets to be too much. Another good site is **excessaccess.com** which matches your stuff with nonprofits in your area that need your stuff.

A note about keys: Keep every key, large and small, new and old, that you find until the end of your sorting and cleaning process. A small key may look like nothing at first. Then you may find a locked suitcase or home security box. You will be glad to have a pile of keys on hand then!

Special note: Nonprofit agencies, thrift stores and charitable institutions vary from city to city and state to state. Everything listed in the following pages is a guideline, put together from the best sources I could survey and research. With any local agency I follow this rule:

When in doubt, check it out!

A phone call can sometimes save a wasted trip made more stressful by returning home with the carload you left with. But, by and large, most of what follows should be pretty universal.

Sorting room by room

Animals and Related Items

Orphaned animals - If an animal has been "orphaned," you hope that prior arrangements have been made for its continued care. If they have, be sure to round up all items related to the animal for the new owner. These include bed, blankets, bedding, food, vitamins and medications, veterinary/vaccination records, licensing records, permits, collar/harness, leash, food, water bowls, heat lamp, travel carrier, cage, kennel, dog house, shelter, toys, nail clippers, litter box and litter.

If no plans have been made, or perhaps you are dealing with an unexpected death, and you are stumped, DO NOT, under any circumstances leave the animal behind in the apartment, house, garage or yard or put it out on the street. Local animal shelters, a humane society or local animal rescue groups can be found online. Animal rescue organizations and shelters often accept not only dogs and cats but other small mammals, rodents, birds and reptiles. Some even accept farm animals and livestock.

Animal-related items left over from past pets are welcomed by animal shelters and pet rescue organizations. Donation wish lists often include beds, bedding, new or used blankets, towels, collars, harnesses, leashes, food and food/water dishes, litter and litter boxes, kennels and dog houses, travel crates, scratching posts, shampoo, brushes, toys, treats, rungs and new carpet scraps. Please donate only those items that are clean and nearly new. You should call ahead to see if there is a demand for small animal and bird cages. Empty fish

32

bowls and aquariums should be sent to a local thrift store; they also make great yard sale items.

Aquariums and Fish

Finding a new home for a full, working aquarium is a bit of a challenge. It might be accepted by a variety of places including child or senior daycare, medical clinics or even a specialty pet store. Always CALL FIRST. The recipient must be willing to accept responsibility for the fish and maintenance and cleaning of the tank. Be sure to discuss who will move the entire setup. If all else fails, look online under 'pets' or 'aquariums' for a store that carries aquariums. They should be able to help you. Goldfish or guppies in a bowl may be best given to a neighbor child. Be sure to ASK the parents first.

Appliances - large

Appliances that are not in good working order belong in one of two places — the dump or a salvage/recycling center. Look online for centers that might haul off old freezers, refrigerators and the like. You may find newspaper classified ads for someone who will haul the item off for a reasonable price. For those items that are in GOOD working order, some charitable thrift stores accept them, some do not.

Note: charitable organizations often DO NOT have staff, volunteers or funds to handle repairs no matter how small the repair and how new the item. When calling agencies about large appliance donations be sure to inquire whether or not pickup service is available.

Habitat for Humanity often comes to mind for appliances, especially refrigerators and built-ins. The agency does NOT accept ANY used appliances for the homes they build. They want to provide new homeowners with new appliances, complete with warranties. Some local chapters will take used appliances and more for resale if they operate a local RESTORE location. Proceeds from sale of items at RESTORE are used to buy materials for new homes. Call before you haul! Some RESTORE locations offer pickup for larger donations but you may have to wait a couple of weeks until a place on the schedule is open.

Here is a list of common large appliances and what type of other organization might be able to use them:

- Refrigerator or freezer – emergency food pantries, group homes, day care centers, domestic violence shelters, agencies that offer transitional housing or refugee resettlement programs.
- Washer and Dryer – agencies that place immigrants, refugee families, domestic violence victims or homeless families into transitional housing units or apartments. Check first with shelters and group homes to see if they accept appliances that are not of commercial grade. Sometimes those made for family use wear out too fast and are not accepted.
- Stoves, ovens and dishwashers – those that are built-in are usually good only for salvage, even if they are in working order. Free standing might be useable by the same agencies listed under washer and dryer above. The same goes for microwaves, although many thrift stores accept microwaves while rejecting other types of ovens.

Appliances - small

Small appliances are often the number-one requested items by charities that operate thrift stores as long as they are in GOOD WORKING ORDER and include cords! As with large appliances, charities do not have staff, volunteers or money to fix items, no matter how new or fancy. Items most requested include:

- mixers WITH beaters
- coffee makers WITH carafes
- toasters
- blenders
- crockpots
- electric frying pans
- toaster ovens

Make sure all parts are included and cord is attached! Mixers without beaters, coffee makers without carafes, crock pots without cords, blenders without lids should be thrown away. Honestly, would you go shopping for parts for one of these items? If you wouldn't, then a customer at a thrift store certainly won't.

Arts and Crafts Supplies

Elementary schools, preschools, churches, scout and 4-H groups, and nonprofit organizations that work with children in after-school or counseling programs can never get enough art supplies. Besides items usually thought of such as paper, colored pencils and markers, they often welcome fabric, yarn, glue and glue sticks, scrap pieces of wood, odd buttons, beads, pipe cleaners, chalk, paints and brushes, shells and small jars or plastic containers for crafts as well as storage.

If the person was an artist and left professional supplies – fancy brushes, oil and acrylic paints, charcoals and blank canvases, call a local high school, community college or university art department. If they can't use the supplies directly for their program perhaps they have a struggling student who would welcome additional materials, especially if they are free.

Art work – pictures, paintings, sculptures, framed posters

This category runs the gamut. Most family art consists of fairly inexpensive pieces that were purchased at craft fairs, furniture, department and big box stores. These items are best put in yard sales or donated to a charity thrift store. Better pieces may be accepted at consignment stores or possibly be accepted by a charity for auction. If you think something might be of significant monetary value, here are some tips before hauling it to a local gallery or specialty store.

For paintings and sculptures, take a picture. Then photograph or make careful notes of any markings in, around, on the back, or bottom of the piece. Can you make out the artist's name from the signature, or is there a signature at all? If a lithograph, or numbered print or limited edition copy has been made, a signature and number, something like 51/200, which means the print is #51 of the 200 made, will be on the mat. Sculptures may have special markings underneath or on the back of the base.

After you have gathered this information, look online under galleries or art dealers and call to ask if they have an appraiser on site or can recommend one. You may also want to look online for a place that specializes in the work of this artist and browse the online catalog to get an idea of various piece's value.

Note: Appraisals are not given over the phone, nor are they free in person. A reputable gallery, that specializes in the type of art you have, e.g. Western, will usually extend the courtesy of looking at your photos and telling you whether it is worth paying to have the piece appraised. Please make an appointment first. Some appraisers will come to your home for a fee after reviewing your photos. If you must have the piece appraised at the gallery, discuss the best way to get it to the gallery, if it is particularly fragile or overly large. Discuss whether the estate will pay transportation and appraisal costs.

Framed movie, event and theater posters are sometimes collectable items. You will need to do some research on the web, or call around to see if there is a memorabilia store in town that buys and sells the type of item you have. Unframed posters of any kind are more often than not yard or thrift store items.

One note about art: Your relative may have been a prolific artist painting numerous pictures, making sculptures or creating ceramics. Family members often think that their relative's art is the greatest, as they should! But, unless your relative's art has been shown in local galleries or sold on the commercial market and her name has a following, don't presume that a gallery or local shop will be interested in selling her art. Art is very subjective and the market is very competitive. Only contact a dealer if you are fairly certain there is a market outside of your family for the pieces.

Assistive Medical Items and Devices

These include canes, walkers, wheelchairs, portable bedside toilets, raised toilet seats, shower chairs, non-slip bath mats, and hospital beds. Call your local Department of Aging, a local hospice or rest home. They may know of a local organization or an individual who is in need of what you have. Other organizations that may have a use for these items are those that work with cancer patients, AIDS patients, people with physical disabilities or the homebound elderly.

Backyard Items

Patio furniture

Some patio furniture can double as inside furniture. If yours qualifies, see guidelines for donating furniture. Other patio furniture could be used by domestic violence shelters, transitional housing, or day centers for seniors or those with disabilities that have yards, patios or decks. Thrift stores may take these items during the spring and summer when they can be easily sold. Most do not have a place to store outdoor furniture through the off-season.

Picnic tables

Picnic tables may be useful at the organizations listed above. Call first. Depending on the size and condition of your picnic table it could also be used as a craft or work table at a youth center.

Barbeque grills

These are tricky and may best be thrown out or given to a neighbor. Because of the hazards of grills fueled by small propane tanks, they cannot be accepted by thrift stores. Charities cannot even transport them in their donation pickup tricks. Charcoal grills, both freestanding and table top, as well as small hibachis might be accepted, but you will need to call first, and they MUST be free of rust. Before donating any type of grill, you MUST empty it of old charcoal and ashes and thoroughly clean it. That includes the greasy rack and inside of the lid. If that is too much work, look for a neighbor who needs a grill, put it out on the curb with a "free sign" if allowed in your neighborhood and hope it disappears, or throw it out.

Play equipment

Swing sets, play houses, plastic climbing cubes and the like are used by daycare centers, domestic violence shelters, preschool, kids clubs IF they meet modern safety standards. If they don't, not even a thrift store will accept them as a donation. When donating a swing set, make sure all the pieces are there. No one will accept a set that is missing one swing and the slide, or that is missing a few bolts. Clean everything before donating, and if the item is a rust bucket, recycle it or have it hauled to the dump. Your best bet might be to ask around the neighborhood.

Bathroom Items

Cosmetics, Perfume and Aftershave

Throw away any cosmetics that have been opened and used — even once. For health reasons, these cannot be used by another person or given away by any organization. That means everything from lipstick to face powder, face cream to deodorant goes into the trash. It should go without saying that anything unopened that has separated, is off-color or looks strange in any way should also be thrown out. Check expiration dates and throw anything that has expired, regardless of appearance. Your mantra here is "When in doubt, throw it out."

New cosmetic items, including samples, are often welcomed for use by schools with drama departments or community theater groups. Organizations that work with low-income women entering the job market, victims of domestic violence, at-risk or incarcerated females of all ages appreciate general cosmetics.

Hygiene Items

Basic unopened hygiene items, including sample and travel sizes, are in big demand by those working with low-income, refugee, marginalized and homeless populations and agencies that work with low-income terminally ill patients. These items include: soap, shampoo, conditioner, lotion, toothbrush and toothpaste, deodorant, disposable razors, new combs and brushes. New or open packages of feminine hygiene items, adult diapers, wet wipes and toilet paper are also great donations. Throw away used brushes and combs. A note about mouthwash: This product may contain high amounts of alcohol unless your state has banned its sale. Mouthwash containing any level of alcohol is not accepted by organizations that deal with youth, at-risk populations and recovering alcoholics.

Electronic Bathroom Appliances

Health regulations prohibit charitable organizations from giving away or selling the following USED items: electric toothbrushes with used toothbrush attachments, waterpicks, oral hygiene equipment, facial steamers, foot baths, personal irrigation systems and similar devices. Charitable thrift stores are happy to accept items such as hair dryers, curling irons, electric curlers, electric razors, heating pads, and lighted makeup mirrors as long as the items are clean, in GOOD working order and include all parts and cords.

Bedding

New sheets, blankets, bedspreads, pillows and cases can be used by homeless shelters, domestic violence shelters and organizations serving refugee and homeless populations. Gently used blankets, sheets, and pillowcases that are clean and in good condition are always needed by organizations that run thrift stores in low-income neighborhoods, and sometimes can be used by agencies that resettle refugees or place homeless families into transitional or permanent housing. Please call first.

Sometimes used items are not accepted if there has been a recent outbreak of bedbugs or similar creatures. Used pillows need to be thrown out! Bedding not good enough for a human charity may be needed at an animal shelter or rescue organization. Some thrift stores sell used sheets and towels to rag factories. This varies widely so again, call first.

Bicycles, Tricycles and Unicycles

Besides donating bikes to thrift stores or putting them in a yard sale, you may find a community group that could use them. Does your community have a bike collective? Tricycles are sometimes on wish lists for centers that serve homeless or abused children or for halfway houses for mothers and children that have outside play areas. You might also consider calling your local Boys and Girls Club or a preschool.

Unless you have CONFIRMED that the agency can perform needed repairs, make sure that bicycles or tricycles can be ridden and their tires are in good shape. If you have bike helmets, knee or elbow pads, please donate them along with your bikes. For bikes that need to be cleaned or need minor repairs, a local bicycle shop may fix the item at no repair if you explain the situation.

Unicycles are specialty items best sold through a local bicycle dealer or on the web.

Books, Magazines and Other Printed Materials

Note: For personal papers and files, paperwork, documents, etc, see Chapter 3.

Books

The primary rule for any book or magazine donation is, Call before you haul.

Libraries accept some books for use by patrons or for resale by groups such as Friends of the Library. CALL FIRST to determine what they will accept and when. Items generally accepted are recently published new and used best-selling fiction, classic and children's literature, books of local historical interest, specialty art books, large print books and manuscripts. Items most often refused include Readers Digest Condensed Books, textbooks, dated travel guides, computer manuals, most magazines and anything with underlining, highlighting, pen, pencil, or crayon markings, in poor condition or missing a front cover. Investing in your local library pays dividends.

Some communities have literacy programs that accept certain types of books. You can also call local charity thrift stores to see if they accept books. Ask if there are certain types of books that are not accepted. These may include old textbooks, Reader's Digest Condensed Books and out-of-date encyclopedias. If you have books you think are of value, call a local independent bookseller to see if they buy used books. If you have numerous books, ask if they will send someone to the house, or ask if you need to bring the books to the store or warehouse. If there is nowhere to resell books locally and you have determined a book collection is of value, and you are from out-of-town, consider if it is worth shipping books home for resale. However, before shipping any books, I highly recommend that you check out resale prices by visiting some of the many websites that sell used books. One of the biggest is Amazon.com. This especially applies to books commonly referred to as coffee table books. These are oversized books with large color pictures throughout. They cost a lot to ship and some are a dime a dozen — not worth nearly what you think they are, despite the beautiful pictures or publication date. When looking online to determine the resale value of certain books, look at the SELLING prices, not the asking prices.

Senior centers, libraries and agencies that work with the sight-impaired are always grateful for donations of large print books and books on tape. Before donating books on tape, make sure the facility has the proper machine on which to play the recordings. If an organization does not have a cassette player, books on cassettes are unwanted donations. Some might accept the donation if it comes with a working tape player. Elementary schools, after-school reading programs and day care centers are good places to donate children's books.

Religious texts such as Bibles, Qurans, related study guides, meditation books etc. are welcome donations at most churches, mosques or synagogues. Consider donating related religious items too. Prisons are another place where religious books are appreciated. These must be new with no markings.

Books relating to religious or fraternal organizations such as Masons, Shriners, Eastern Star, Knights of Columbus, P.E.O., Moose or Elks, should be returned to the organization, if possible. If someone in the family was an active member, there should be a directory around the house. Call the organization president for instructions. Don't forget to also return pins, robes, rings, aprons and other ceremonial or sacred items.

Specialty books

Was your relative a doctor, teacher, regional historian, attorney? Here are some rules of thumb and suggestions for dealing with these items.

Old textbooks — primarily those of general nature less than 80 years old — are generally of no use to anyone. You should recycle or throw them out. Very, very old textbooks may be of value for their humor or some unique historical perspectives. Check with a local educational institution or independent bookseller to see if this might be the case. Technical textbooks relating to medicine, law or advancing sciences are usually of no use after two years; computer texts are obsolete almost as soon as they are printed. No one will buy them; no one wants them as a donation. Out they go! Sometimes a recycling outlet will take them.

Technical reports, research papers, maps, or manuscripts may have value to others in the field. Contact a local college or university for suggestions on who could use these items. On occasion a local antique store may buy papers or old maps of interest in the local community.

Magazines

These need to be considered carefully! Before packing them up and hauling them to the library or putting them out for a yard sale, here are a few things to consider. Old issues of widely circulated, time-sensitive magazines such as *TIME* and *People* are generally of no use as reading material for schools or libraries except those that cover key historic events. A local history teacher may value those issues. It seems like every family must have saved a copy of Life with historical photos on the cover — the JFK assassination or man landing on the moon. There are so many out there that even these magazines are of little monetary value. Again, see if a history teacher might want them. And the rest? Throw them out or send them to recycling. With the plethora of pictures now available on electronic devices, fewer organizations want to store paper copies any more.

National Geographic magazines are not usually accepted by used book stores or libraries. Their colorful pictures are great for art projects at schools, faith communities and youth centers, or by youth groups such as Boy and Girl Scouts. Other widely read magazines such as Woman's Day are best donated to the aforementioned groups for craft projects. Specialty magazines that contain lots of recipes or patterns for knitting, woodworking etc. are often good yard sale items. Libraries may accept specialty magazines that focus on local history, architecture or general regional sports such as skiing or sailing. Always Call First! And, when in doubt, throw it out! Considering recycling? See Chapter 1 for suggestions.

"How to" pamphlets, travel brochures, city and subway maps are junk, unless a family member wants to keep them for sentimental reasons. Don't donate them to a library or thrift store. They will just have to throw them out, so do them a favor and dispose of these items yourself.

Camping Items

Groups that serve homeless individuals living on the streets are always in need of sleeping bags, backpacks, and foam sleeping mats. They can often use tents of any size, lanterns, flashlights and batteries, charcoal, portable stoves and sometimes firewood. Check to see if you have a local chapter of Volunteers of America, Salvation Army or a similar group in your area that does homeless outreach or case management. Boy or Girl Scout troops may be in need of some of these items too. In many areas troops can no longer cut firewood and have to bring their own on camp-outs. Ask a scout leader about taking firewood, as long as it's not infested with termites! For suggestions on items like canoes, sailboats, kayaks and rubber rafts see the sports equipment section later in this chapter.

Cars, Trucks, Campers, Travel Trailers, Recreational Vehicles, ATVs, Motorized Boats and Jet skis

So no one in the family wants the folks' 1978 motorhome or mom's old jalopy? Now what? If you are short on time and just want to donate it, go to **donateacar.com**. You can click on your state and get a list of state and national organizations that accept cars, campers, RVs and boats. There are answers to frequently asked questions, a donation form you can download and a toll free number to ask a real person more questions. For those without computer access call 1-800-237-5714. The charity may even send a tow truck to pick up something that doesn't run. Auto tow trucks will sometimes pick up non-operational vehicles, often free of charge.

For those with time and desire to sell the vehicle themselves, first call a bank, credit union or car dealer for the blue book price. They will give you a low and high value for the vehicle so you know how much to charge and what you can expect to get. Check the newspaper and online classified ads to see what others are charging for a comparable vehicle. If you want to sell the car to a dealer, clean it up and shop it around. There can be a difference of hundreds of dollars between dealers. For the sake of everyone involved, set a "shop around" deadline, or limit your visits to two or three dealers. Accept that you have covered the bases that time allows, sell the vehicle, and move on.

Whether selling or donating a car, trailer, RV or boat, be sure to check around the garage and house for items to throw in with the deal. These could include new cans of oil, washer fluid, fuses, spare tires, extra floor mats, life jackets, tow ropes or tie downs. Let prospective buyers know if ATVs, jet skis or sailboats DO NOT come with trailers. Buyers will expect those to be included unless you state otherwise.

IMPORTANT NOTE: Before selling any vehicle you must have the title, information on any outstanding loan and proof that you have legal authority to sell. Most people keep free and clear titles to their cars in a safe deposit box or home safe, however I have found titles in dresser drawers, under mattresses, and in piles of papers mixed in with old mail, bills, shopping lists and coupons, among other places! If the title has been lost, contact your state Department of Motor Vehicles about obtaining a duplicate title. If the vehicle has an outstanding loan the lien holder will be holding the title. This also applies to most other types of recreational toys.

Chemicals, Caustic Cleaners, Old Paint, Explosives

Call your local health department to find out how to properly dispose of any harmful substances. If you find any particularly dangerous chemicals or acids, call the fire department non-emergency number. They may need to send a hazardous material disposal crew to your home. In the case of something extremely unstable such as partially decayed dynamite, DO NOT attempt to move it. Call authorities immediately. NEVER throw any items of this type into regular trash containers or dumpsters!

While clearing an estate we found several cases of partially decayed dynamite and called the local police to ask what we should do. They sent an officer to verify what we had found and subsequently the ATF was mobilized to take the stuff away – after evacuating surrounding houses! We were quite the spectacle! At another estate, we thought we had a similar situation on our hands. However, the investigating officer determined that the boxes contained old road flares. He helped us dispose of them on site and the neighbors were none the wiser.

Clothing

Before donating clothing first answer these questions for each item:
1. Is it clean? Is it free of pet hair?
2. Is it in good repair? Are all buttons there, and does the zipper work? Is the garment free of holes, tears or stains?
3. For shoes, are they free of holes in the tops or bottoms? Are the heels in

good repair? Are the laces there?

In short, if it fit and was your style, would YOU wear it?

If the answer to any of these questions is NO, throw the item away! Otherwise the charity on the receiving end will have to do it, which wastes valuable time and resources. One of the biggest overhead expenses charity thrift stores incur is dumpster fees. If you truly support your local charitable thrift store throw out your OWN damaged clothing.

Charity thrift shops affiliated with large, national organizations accept all types of used clothing, suits, pantyhose and socks, shoes, sweaters and coats, hats, gloves and scarves, accessories (belts, purses, jewelry), slips, bras and long underwear. For health reasons used underpants, briefs and boxers cannot be resold.

If you decide to take clothes to collection bins in a shopping center parking lot, be aware that these bins may NOT be connected to charity thrift shops or will somehow help the needy. They could be connected to for-profit salvage operations that turn clothes into rags or sell them to developing countries. In this case, your donation may not be tax deductible.
A reputable charity will be able to supply you with a donation receipt upon pick-up or when you deliver items to the store. Check hours of operation before you haul.

General work uniforms, special work clothing (all weather coveralls) or footwear (steel-toed boots) are also accepted by charitable thrift stores. They are also useful in programs that help people get back to work.

Old Scout uniforms may be of interest to the local chapter. Contact a local veteran's organization for suggestions on who might like old military uniforms and other war memorabilia. One nationwide organization is Veterans of Foreign Wars.

Old wedding dresses, tuxedos, fancy evening wear and period pieces are sometimes considered vintage clothing. Look for listings under vintage clothing to see if there are any stores in your area that buy these items. Sometimes these items are taken by consignment shops. Junior and High Schools with large numbers of low income students often collect clothing, shoes and jewelry for school dances and proms.

Consider donating costumes and period pieces, including hats and accessories to a local school drama club or community theater group.

Wedding dresses are accepted by thrift stores. Yours may make a dream come true.

I volunteered at a community thrift store for many years. One day a young woman came in to shop and was admiring a wedding dress that had just been donated. She mentioned that she was engaged, and was to be married at the county building wedding "room." Her dream had always been a church wedding but she wasn't doing that because she could not afford a beautiful dress in which to walk down the aisle. The dress looked like it would fit her; we encouraged her to try it on. It fit perfectly! She shyly asked how much it was. We asked her how much she had. Only $25 she answered. The store manager said, "Well that's how much it is!" She bought the dress, saying she was going home to call her fiancé, her mom and dad, and the church. She was beaming through her tears as she left. We were all in tears too. What a great new life for an old wedding dress!

Collectables and Collections

Most people tend to start collections at some point in their lives. Just because someone collected certain items doesn't mean those items are of great value — or any value at all — to anyone but an avid collector. How do you determine if items have large monetary value? How do you find a dealer or collector in your area? Below are a few ideas to get you started.

If you are dealing with a collection that you need to have appraised, call or visit a local dealer who specializes in the type of item you have to see if they will come in, appraise and perhaps even buy the collection. This includes fine art, antique furniture, coin and stamp collections and can run the gamut. Especially when dealing with stamps and coins, there may be just a few items of higher value and the rest are of face value. Only a knowledgeable dealer can tell you for sure. Dealers are listed in local yellow pages or online under their respective headings.

For items like figurines, glassware, collectable dishes e.g. Christmas plates, first look on the bottom and write down any company name, pattern or figure name, country in which the item was produced, series name and year produced if one in a series, any numbers (40/125) or markings (crown, seahorse, shamrock). Measure the height or diameter of each item. Call or email this information to a local dealer or resale/consignment store to see if the item has any significant value. If not, you may want to donate it to a local thrift store.

Thimbles, souvenir spoons, salt-and-pepper shakers, bottles and the like run the gamut from junk to perhaps true collectables. Make a list of what is unique about each item and note the size of each item. Note if the item is still in its original packaging and whether the packaging has been opened. This is especially important when determining the value of toys.

Sports memorabilia also runs the gamut. Check online sites that specialize in items like baseball cards. Collections of local team memorabilia are best advertised on local classified sites.

From here you have two options.

1.　On your home computer, or computer with free online service at your local library, look up a large online auction website. One of the biggest is www.ebay.com. You can search for items by category (thimbles, figurines) and see what prices are being offered for the same or similar items. You can also search by corporate name for items widely collected. These include collectables exclusively manufactured by worldwide companies such as Waterford. Amazon and Yahoo, among others, also host online auction sites.

NOTE – if you are new to online auction sites, be aware that the price often listed with the item is the seller's asking price, not always a true indication of the item's value. To see if the item is in demand and priced right, look at the number of bids it has received, if any, and what the highest current bid is. Odds are that an item up for auction for a long period of time with no bids isn't even worth the asking price. Remember, these sites are only guides to value and should not be used in determining what you might get selling your items online, at a local store, flea market or yard sale.

2.　Look online for a local antique or secondhand shop to inquire about your items. Someone who has been in the business awhile can tell you if you have something valuable or of little resale value. The latter items can safely be given to a thrift store or put in your yard sale. You might consider donating items a bit nicer than thrift or yard sale to a local nonprofit organization or faith community for an upcoming rummage sale, auction or other fundraising event.

While general inquiries over the phone can determine what dealers will consider buying, store owners will need to see items to give you a fair and accurate evaluation. Before packing and hauling large collections or fragile items around town, consider taking some digital pictures of a few choice items and taking them to the dealer. This saves unnecessary work and also avoids possible breakage of valuable items. Take photos of each item from several angles and include photos of the back or bottom if it includes special markings, numbers or other important information. Be sure to also take your notes listing special markings, numbers and measurements. The more information, the better.

Owners of local second-hand stores who are not interested in seeing or buying your collection may know of locals who are. They may be able to give you contact information for someone interested in buying part or all of the collection. Sometimes they may also know of local groups whose members collect a specific item such as beer bottles, matchbooks, or buttons. You might also look around the house for newsletter or specialty magazines published for collectors of a certain type of specialty object.

Natural items collected by professionals, such as rocks, fossils, or butterflies may be useful to a local college or university professor. Unless your item is a rare and has been professionally preserved/mounted, museums are not interested in taking them as part of their collections. Otherwise, beauty is in the eye of the collector. Call local youth centers or groups to see if shells, driftwood, etc. can be used for arts and crafts projects. Maybe a neighbor kid would be thrilled to receive some colorful shells or rocks. Use your best judgment here. When in doubt, throw it out!

I've dealt with estates that have bequeathed collections of seashells, pot shards, or rocks to museums. The heirs pack them up, haul them to the museum only to be told that not only did the museum not ask for or pre-approve the donation, they have no space to store the collection and, by the way, the collection isn't worth much to anyone except perhaps an amateur who likes that kind of thing.

Computers, Tablets, Software, Scanners, Printers and Related Items

Computers older than one year are considered obsolete. So is software that goes with them. Computer games are tricky, too. Use the same rule of thumb as for software. A computer manufactured in the last two years may be able to be upgraded so that new software and accessories can be used with it, but the cost may be more than all the items are worth. Anything older cannot be upgraded. Keyboards, printers, tablets, readers, and similar items may be useful for a bit longer. Monitors that are not flat screens, computer mouses (mice?) that are not wireless are obsolete. For those unfamiliar with computer vintages, find someone who knows how to determine the features of the system before considering donating it to any organization. If you are unfamiliar with computers and on your own, write down the manufacturer and model number and call a local computer dealer. Or you can always ask a teen in the neighborhood!

5 1/4" floppy and 3 ½" hard disks are now obsolete, as are rewritable blank disks, are of no use, unless you need some coasters for drinks or plants.

Curtains, Blinds and Shutters

Curtains are great thrift store items. You should include the hooks or rings needed to hang them. If you decide to give away the curtain rods be sure all hardware and pulls are included with the rods. Put all long pieces together in a large box or secure them together with packing or duct tape. Place small screws and brackets in a Ziploc bag, and then tape to the bundled rods. Blinds can also be donated to thrift stores, but only if they work and you include all cords, mounting brackets and hardware.

Shutters are often custom items. Call ahead to see if local thrift stores take these items. If you donate shutters be sure all mounting brackets, screws, etc. are included. Put all these items in a Ziploc bag and securely attach it to the shutters.

Dishes, Kitchenware and Miscellaneous Kitchen Items

Every non-electronic item in the kitchen from dishes and silverware, pots and pans or mixing bowl, is accepted by most charity thrift stores. It doesn't matter if dish sets are not complete or that forks don't match spoons as long as everything is clean and useable. Many basic kitchen items are also in high demand by charities that set up apartments for formerly homeless clients or refugees being resettled in the area.

Small electric appliances such as coffee makers, crockpots, or toasters, should be donated only if they are in working order, clean, complete, and include power cords that are not frayed or otherwise unsafe. Very old electrical appliances are often fire hazards. Take them to someplace that recycles electronics if possible, otherwise throw them out. The same rules apply to microwave and toaster ovens. Coffee makers should include glass carafes. Water purification devices should have old filters removed.

Nonprofits are happy to have paper bags, paper products (plates, napkins, towels), plastic silverware, tinfoil, self seal bags etc. in packages that have been opened as long as everything inside is clean and not too old. Partial rolls of plastic wrap and tinfoil are fine too. Please recycle or throw away previously used plastic bread bags and ties, tinfoil, etc. As much as your relative loved to save that stuff, it cannot be passed on to anyone else unless you want to take it home. This also applies to pieces of string, rubber bands, and similar odds and ends often found in kitchen drawers.

Small and medium baskets make great thrift store items. Large, well-made baskets can sometimes be used by groups for putting auction items in. Call ahead before hauling.

Many churches are in need of vases; larger vases for flower arrangements and smaller vases for flowers taken to the homebound or those who are ill.

Canning jars may be useful to county extension programs, 4H groups, or community garden projects.

Misc. containers - Plastic containers that have name brands like Tupperware or Rubbermaid are good thrift store items with or without lids. Containers that previously held food items, e.g. cottage cheese, yogurt or sour cream, even though clean, need to be recycled, donated to a group for use in craft projects, or thrown away. This also applies to glass jars. Some thrift stores accept clean metal cookie tins and gift boxes that do NOT have company names on the lids. Old coffee cans, with or without lids should also be recycled. For china, crystal glasses and dishes, or silver flatware and dishes, call a local dealer, look online as described in the 'Collectables' section. You can also look at going rates for china, crystal and silver online. Good sites include **www. edish.com** for china and **www.replacements.com** for china, crystal glassware and silver flatware.

Electronics - including Home Office Machines

Most electronic items are accepted by charitable thrift stores on two conditions: they work, and they are not obsolete. Charities do NOT have staff or volunteers that are able to repair electronic items, no matter how good or new they are, nor do they have money in the budget to purchase parts to fix any donations. Items including flat screen TVs, DVD players, portable electronic music players could also be donated to group homes or shelters. Sometimes stores that sell LP and 45 records buy and resell old phonographs. In general, obsolete items to be junked include reel-to-reel and 8-track tape players, VCR players and old tube TVs. If you are in a larger metropolitan area there may be a recycling facility for those types of items. There is usually a fee to recycle old TVs.

Some of you may be cleaning out a home office or study with older electronic office equipment. Old adding machines and typewriters, both electronic and manual, have almost no market, either free or monetary. This also applies to old handheld electronic organizers and calculators. Most charitable thrift shops will not even accept these items, so call before you haul. If you feel the item may be a true antique with possible monetary value, get online and check it out. There may be an off chance that a local theater group could use your old typewriter as a prop.

You can also go online and find numerous cell phone recycling companies. Some manufacturers will take your old phone back for recycling or possible credit towards a newer version. I have had good success selling cell phones with **Gazelle.com**. They will give you an immediate quote, send you a prepaid shipping label, send you payment in a number of ways or let you contribute your proceeds to charity.

See earlier section for information on computers and related items.

Exercise Equipment

This is a tough one. Sometimes a senior recreation center or youth activity center may be able to use a piece of equipment. Try advertising online classified site. Be sure to make it clear if delivery is included or pickup is required. In many areas you will be lucky if you can find someone who will just come and take the equipment off your hands!

It can be worth the cost to have professional movers or those who deliver and set up exercise equipment come and remove your items. One client let people who had no idea what they were doing come to move a very heavy exercise bicycle, complete with electronic screen. The stairs were narrow, and a bit steep. Halfway to the landing the bicycle slipped and went right through the wall at the turn in the staircase. Three days before closing on their house, the sellers had to get a handyman in to put up sheetrock, patch, and paint. It came down to the wire. Not what you need when trying to move!

Eyeglasses

Lions Club International collects eyeglasses in numerous communities throughout the country. Donation boxes can be found at some national chain eyeglass companies or local community collection points such as libraries. The Lions Club accepts any type prescription eyeglasses, single and bifocal, as well as prescription sunglasses. Check with your local club to see if loose prescription lenses are ever accepted. Many chapters do NOT accept used glasses cases. **Lionsclubs.org**

Fabric, Patterns, and Sewing Supplies

Larger pieces of fabric can be used by a variety of groups. Call a local church or senior center to inquire about quilting groups. Local youth groups such as Girl Scouts or 4H may also be involved in making quilts for service projects. These groups might also need straight pins, scissors, and other sewing supplies. Ask if they can use craft sewing patterns for stuffed animals or decorative items for fundraising events. I have yet to find any organization that can use general sewing patterns for dresses, etc. For suggestions on donating related items, such as buttons, lace, and fabric scraps see the arts and crafts supplies section. For sewing machines see suggestions later in this chapter.

Food

While intentions are always good in thinking that food should not be wasted, please help the recipient organization by being aware of the following:

NO food in open containers can be given out or reused by a charitable organization serving humans for health reasons. This includes condiments in the refrigerator, catsup, soy sauce, tartar sauce etc. Throw away very old spices and seasonings, too.

Cans with severe dents, missing labels, or that have puffed out lids cannot be given away, also for health reasons. Throw these out!

Food that is individually packaged such as granola bars, but in an open box, can be given away, as long as the internal packaging is intact.

Special diet foods – low salt, diabetic snacks, nutrition drinks are always in demand at food pantries, food banks and some programs that serve homebound seniors or terminally ill patients.

Frozen, canned or bottled foods that have not been commercially packaged cannot be accepted by charitable organizations. If donating frozen foods, call ahead to make sure the agency has a freezer and freezer space. Throw out anything with freezer burn.

Open bags of unexpired dry pet food can be used by animal shelter and rescue organizations. Some opened food items, such as grains, may also be accepted if the organization cares for unusual animals such as poultry. In some areas farmers are happy to take old unopened cans of wheat and other grains to use as pig feed.

Formal wear and wedding dresses

See specialty clothing in CLOTHING section earlier in this chapter.

Fur Coats, Wraps, Muffs

In this age of vegetarians and PETA, there is not a large demand for these items as in past decades. There are however, people who still desire furs in any form. Large resale markets have developed in vintage clothing stores. Look online for stores nearby. You might also look online for a local furrier who might be interested in buying older furs, in good condition, or they might steer you to someone who might be interested in your items. Some pieces may also make good costumes. Contact your local school drama club or community theater to determine if they can use anything you might have.

Furniture

Many charitable thrift stores take furniture of any size and kind. However, some do not, due to space limitations. One item always REFUSED is a used mattress. For health reasons, stores do not and cannot accept them. See if there is a mattress recycling outlet in your area. For other ideas about what to do with old mattresses go to www.tuck.com/mattress-disposal.

Remember that all donations must be clean, in good condition, good repair and be complete. Charities do not have time or money to repair broken pieces or equipment to steam clean upholstery.

Consignment is an option for nicer and vintage furniture items, as well as some vintage decorative items and fancy dishes. Here are the questions to ask when calling a consignment store.

Do you come to the house to inspect items free of charge?

Do I need to send you pictures first?

Do you have pick-up service available and at what cost?

How long do you keep items?

What percentage of each sale do you keep?

Do you ever mark things down? When, and by how much? Is it with or without my permission?

What happens to unsold items when my consignment contract expires? If those items go to charity will I get a donation receipt?

Guns, Ammunition and Explosives

The first thing to be sure of when dealing with any gun is that you know how to handle it properly. If, for any reason, you are not sure how to safely handle the firearm in question, call your local police department. Guns can appear to be unloaded and still have a round in the chamber. Improper handling could lead to injury or death. Police officers are ALWAYS willing to send someone to your house to deal with any weapon you have found. This goes for all guns, new or very old. It is best to err on the side of safety.

I found a gun while cleaning out the house of a deceased acquaintance. It was very small, black and quite old. It looked like a toy but not wanting to take chances I called the police. The officer arrived and determined that the gun was an old "Saturday Night Special", a real gun indeed. Upon further examination he determined that there was one bullet left in the gun, loaded into the chamber. I was thankful that it was checked out and removed from the property by a law enforcement officer. Think of the tragedy if it had been donated, as a toy, to a thrift store and someone had been injured or killed. It bears repeating, err on the side of safety.

Reselling guns can be tricky, so can taking or shipping firearms home across state lines. There are states where all private gun ownership is illegal and so, reselling a firearm locally is in violation of the law. There are also states where private ownership of certain types of guns, handguns, for example, is illegal. This may prohibit a family member from taking a family firearm home. Some states, such as California, require that all guns be sold through licensed dealers and putting a rifle into a yard sale would be against the law. If you are unsure of local or state laws, call your local police or sheriff department NON-EMERGENCY number found in the government pages of the phone book or online. Shipping guns must be done through licensed gun dealers. Do not ship guns through local mail or national package delivery services.

If you happen upon unused ammunition that you don't know how to handle or dispose of, this also necessitates a call to the police. They will pick it up and dispose of it safely or instruct you in how to properly dispose of your items. NEVER throw unused ammunition in your home garbage containers or a community dumpster. This is very dangerous and can lead to harmful consequences if the wrong person gets hold of it. There are also stiff fines if you are caught disposing of ammunition, gunpowder, explosive devices or firecrackers in an unsafe manner.

Unused fireworks are accepted at any local fire department. In more rural areas call someone who volunteers with the local department for help in properly disposing of any of the items listed above.

For those dealing with reloading equipment, call a local gun dealer to see if they handle resale of these types of items. NEVER throw out gunpowder used in reloading; follow the suggestions above.

On the chance that you come across dynamite, blasting caps, or anything that looks like a grenade, bomb, or loaded shell casing, call the police or local ATF unit immediately, and stay clear of these items until proper authorities arrive. This also goes for any chemical compounds that look unstable.

Hangers

This has been the subject of an ongoing nationwide discussion among professional organizers. Responsible hanger disposal is almost an oxymoron. Most thrift stores do not accept hanger donations of any kind; a few will accept the tubular plastic variety because they can sell them. Wire hangers cannot be recycled and dry cleaners, where most of these hangers come from, very rarely take them back for reuse. There needs to be a nationwide effort to encourage dry cleaners to take back these hangers, clean them and reuse them. Another hanger problem is with retail stores. Whether the clothing comes from a big box store, a department store or a specialty boutique, the stores where I shop almost always MAKE me take the hanger, even if I tell them to keep it! I don't care if the item is put in a shopping bag and gets wrinkled before I get home. For items like exercise clothes, who cares! I throw away hundreds of pounds of clients' hangers every year. Even the local refugee resettlement program is so overrun with hangers they won't even take the nicest ones I have to offer. Unless you get lucky and find someone on a neighborhood freecycle site, your hangers will end up in the landfill.

Hearing Aids

Some communities are lucky enough to have hearing aid recycling centers. Lions Club International operates hearing aid recycling centers in some states. To find out if yours is one, visit **www.lionsclub.org**. Senior centers may know of an individual who is in need of your donation. When donating hearing aids be sure to include any packages of unused, unexpired batteries.

Heating and Cooling Equipment

Space heaters, room heaters, window and portable air conditioners, electric fans are always in big demand by organizations that work with elderly and low income clients. Call around to see who can use what. Donate one of these items only if it is in good working order, it is clean, it is up to code (not too old), it includes a cord and the cord is not frayed, spliced or repaired in any way. Home improvement thrift stores also accept these items as long as they are in working order!

Household Cleaners and Cleaning Supplies

Many charitable organizations willingly accept open containers of cleaning products that are not too old. This includes kitchen and laundry detergent. New sponges and mops, gently used brooms, dustpans and buckets are great too! Used mops, sponges, scrubbers, dust rags should be thrown out, Old cleaners and polishes should be disposed of properly. Call your local health department for directions on how and where to properly dispose of toxic cleaning materials.

Holiday Items

Holiday decorations and dishes can be among the most sentimental items you will deal with. Christmas tree decorations, Halloween masks, and menorahs can all bring back fond memories. For the most cherished items, you may want to use the Family Lottery method described in Chapter 1. For other items such as Christmas tree ornaments some of which everyone would like, use the Round Robin system, also described in Chapter 1. If your family is more laid-back, put these items on a table when the family gathers for a special occasion or family reunion and tell everyone to help themselves. For the remaining items, consider donating them to a local nursing home, senior center, day care, Boys and Girls Club or center serving low-income families.

Jewelry and Watches

Costume jewelry and everyday watches are great thrift store or yard sale items. If you think a piece is valuable, take it to a reputable jeweler for an appraisal. Note: jewelry appraisals are not free. Check on the cost before leaving the item. Be sure all family members have agreed on who pays the cost and who decides what to leave for appraisal. Chapter 1 lists ideas for coming to consensus on this.

If you are in doubt about whether the stone in an item is a valuable gem or a nice piece of glass, a reputable jeweler will tell you that at no cost. They can also tell you if unusual stones are real or fake and often identify them for you. Local jewelers can often help you with watch valuations. If not, take them to a local specialty watch store.

Linens

Household, bed and bath – sheets, pillowcases, bath towels, washcloths, bathroom rugs, toilet seat covers.

Those that are clean, in good condition and without stains can be given to local charitable thrift shops or agencies that run resettlement programs. Sheets and towels with stains and tears can often be used by a local animal shelter or pet rescue organization. Call first.

Household, everyday kitchen

The same guidelines for household bed and bath apply to kitchen towels. Hot pads and oven mitts, placemats, tablecloths and cloth napkins are also accepted by charities, though not by animal shelters.

Fine linens

Lace runners, tablecloths, crocheted doilies, finely embroidered bed linens and other handcrafted items may be accepted by a local antique, retro or upscale consignment store. The resale market on many of these items is low and very flat. You may have to come to terms with donating these to an upscale thrift boutique.

Liquor

Churches do not accept donations of wine; restaurants and wedding reception centers do not accept alcohol of any kind. The saying, "use it or lose it" definitely applies here.

Luggage

Call a local domestic violence shelter or homeless shelter to see if there is a current need for suitcases, duffle bags, tote bags, or backpacks. Often their clients can use these to move belongings to other housing at a later time, in lieu of trash bags, thus maintaining a sense of dignity. Low-income school children can use kids' backpacks and sometimes tote bags. Some schools can use backpacks, totes or reusable bags for weekend food programs. All of these items, except reusable shopping bags, are generally accepted by thrift stores.

Medical Items and Supplies

These include glucometers, new syringes, alcohol prep pads, sterile pads, latex gloves, blood pressure cuffs and thermometers. Call a local nonprofit health clinic for information on a local program that might be in need of these items. If you are in an area without a clinic, ask around to see if someone in the neighborhood might have a condition such as diabetes. They might be grateful for extra supplies.

Medicines

Prescriptions – Please properly dispose of all medications of this type! Take pills to your local pharmacy or police station. Do NOT flush them down the toilet or put them down the drain and contaminate local water systems. Under no circumstances should prescription medications be passed on to anyone else. There are sometimes rumors that senior centers or public health clinics need them for low income clients. Not only is that false, but giving out prescription medication to any but the person it has been prescribed for is against the law.

THIS IS VITAL in helping curb the national opioid epidemic. If you have been prescribed pain medication, PLEASE dispose of the remaining pills or liquid properly as soon as possible.

IMPORTANT: Prescription medication labels contain lots of personal information that makes them a prime target for identity and drug theft. Identity theft happens to all people, even the deceased. Make sure labels are removed or destroyed before bottles, tubes or boxes are disposed of. If you have trouble removing the label, cross out information with a permanent marker.

Over-the-counter – Any over-the-counter medicines that have been opened, from aspirin to cough syrup should be thrown away in the trash. Empty the contents into the trash and recycle the container where possible.

Distributing new, closed containers of these medications by local nonprofits can sometimes be tricky. There are often ordinances that restrict who can dispense what. Call before taking any items anywhere. Sometimes domestic violence shelters and public clinics can accept donations of basic medications like aspirin or ibuprofen. Again, DO NOT flush medications down the toilet or dispose of them down the sink drain. This contributes to an ever growing problem of water pollution. It is very difficult, if not impossible to get some medications out of local water systems.

Music

Recorded

Records – Look for a used record dealer if you are in a metropolitan area. Vinyl is making a comeback, but don't expect to get anything for a record that has been played a lot, has scratches or is by an artist of less than international fame. Occasionally thrift stores accept them; check first. Some people think that record album covers are valuable. VERY few in the world are worth anything. Do not think that your record collection is going to fund a cruise. It won't!

Tapes – 8-track tapes are junk, as are old reel-to-reel tapes. A few thrift stores will still accept cassettes in cases.

CDs - These are good yard sale items as long as they are commercial recordings. Homemade recordings, even disks burned on your computer, have NO resale value. Throw out sample and demo CDs. They are not recyclable.

Sheet music

Ask a neighbor if someone in the area plays a certain musical instrument for which you have sheet music. You can also try calling a local music store that sells the particular instrument to inquire about teachers in the area. They are often happy to have extra sheet music for their students. Schools are another place to call. Music books with collections of older tunes may be a joy for someone who plays at a local nursing home. If you are giving away an instrument, send sheet music or music books along with the instrument.

Musical Instruments

Pianos and organs are the most common items in this category. Before you decide on what to do with the piano or organ, read the section in Chapter 1, "Who pays for what". That will give you a better idea of which member of the family, if any, will be taking the piano or organ to their home. If you decide to donate it to a school, faith community, or local nonprofit agency, perhaps a senior center, you must decide beforehand if you can offer to include moving as part of the donation. That will be a major factor to many recipient organizations as to whether they can accept such a donation. A senior center will probably not have a truck and personnel who can pick up and move a piano from your house to their location.

Guitars and banjos may be resold through a local dealer. These also sell well online but you must find a case for shipping and a shipping agent who knows how to properly pack and ship instruments.

Wind, brass and string instruments, if not of great value, are often needed for use in school music programs that offer band and orchestra classes, especially in lower income schools and rural communities. Some local music stores buy lower-end musical instruments to use for rentals. Instruments of higher value should be appraised and sold through a reputable dealer, one who specializes in the type of instrument you are trying to sell.

Odd, inexpensive musical and percussion instruments such as recorders, tambourines and castanets, can often be used by preschools and in elementary school programs.

Unusual instruments from foreign countries – check with local refugee groups or friends who are musicians.

Newspapers

If there is no local recycling program for newspapers, try calling your local animal shelter or rescue organization. They often use old newspapers for cage liners or cleaning. Some businesses use them for packing material.

To determine if very old newspapers have historical value, call the local historical society, county museum or your local newspaper office. A history teacher at a local school might appreciate having older newspapers for teaching aids. Your local history museum or historical society may also be interested in newspapers of local historical significance.

Office Furniture and Equipment

Filing cabinets, desks and chairs are great thrift store items or may be useful to any number of charitable organizations. Call around to see who might need what or if there is 2-1-1 helpline in your area, call them for wish lists of local nonprofit organizations. Make sure your local thrift store accepts this type of furniture before you haul it there. If a charity is picking up items at your house, CONFIRM that they will take office furniture. Otherwise you may return home to find that all your other donations have been taken but the desk is still on your front porch!

See previous section COMPUTERS for information on disposing of monitors, printers, Ipads, cables etc. For office items such as typewriters and adding machines see ELECTRONICS – Office Machines section earlier in this chapter.

Local charities, schools or faith communities can use most general office supplies such as paper, pens, notepads, paperclips, file folders. They can often use all-purpose items such as binders, staplers and scissors. It should go without saying that old rubber bands and now obsolete items like typewriter erasers should be thrown away. This also applies to old pens, partially used pencils and pencil leads that do not go with a pencil you are donating.

Paint, Turpentine, Solvents

Call your local health department to ask about proper disposal methods for any substance of this type. Putting these items in a curbside trash can, trash transfer station bag, apartment house dumpster or down your home drain or sewer, is not only dangerous, it is illegal. Fines are steep for those who get caught. You may want to post anything of this nature that is still useable on **Freecycle.org.**

Painting supplies such as NEW brushes, paint pans and liners and drop cloths can be used by a number of organizations. Look in Arts and Crafts section for some ideas. Check around. Throw out used brushes, pans, liners and cheap plastic drop cloths. Heavy canvas commercial-grade drop clothes may still be useful.

Photographs, Slides and Home Movies

Photos

Here is where a sorting system will really saves you! If you have a few great framed photos that everyone wants, use the lottery or round robin system described in Chapter 1. Depending on time, you may wish to give all the photos to one person in the family who can sort them and then send the others a list of what was in the pile. You can also save them until everyone can get together for a holiday or family reunion celebration.

When you are ready to tackle this project, here are some sorting suggestions. Instead of KEEP, GIVE, and THROW, use one or more of the following categories and add your own as needed. Keep negatives and pictures together.

- o Mom, or if two moms, a pile for each
- o Dad, or if two dads, a pile for each
- o Mom and dad/ couple together
- o Mom's side of the family – parents, siblings, cousins – single and group shots
- o Dad's side of the family
- o Family together
- o Scenery
- o Who are these people? (no one present has a clue, but others might)
- o Throw

After sorting pictures into categories, you will have to decide if you need to use the Round Robin or Family Lottery again, as detailed in Chapter 1, for the most desired pictures that do not have negatives. For those with accompanying negatives, decide how many copies to make and decide who will pay for reprints. You may also want to digitize photos and give everyone electronic copies.

For very old family photos sit together and label the back with those in the picture. It may be obvious to you that one picture is your mother when she was 25, but your kids and grandkids won't have a clue. Be sure not to damage the photo by pressing hard on the back or using a marker that will bleed through. I recommend using a very sticky post-it. Or think about writing on labels and then putting them on the back of the picture. Pictures that appear fragile could be put in a labeled envelope.

There may be photos that no one wants but that may be of historical value. They may be of downtown decades ago or have been taken by a prominent local photographer. If you think this might be the case, call the local historical society and ask if someone can look at your pictures. Sometimes old portraits are in demand by decorators going for a vintage feel, not only in a home but at a theme restaurant or hotel.

If they are recent, do not be afraid to throw away pictures in the "Who are these people?" pile. Ask older family members about those you think might be of relatives in their youth. For numerous pictures of very similar scenes, such as the 14 rolls of film taken on the last family trip to Florida in 1982, think about having each family member pick a picture from that trip and throwing the rest away. It may sound a bit ruthless, but you will feel better in the long run. Boxes of family pictures become overwhelming very quickly.

Slides

Use the same initial sorting system described above for photos. The easiest way to sort slides is by using a lighted slide sorting table. If you don't have one, I recommend buying one. They are small tabletop units, fairly inexpensive and are worth every dollar. After the initial sort, using the system above in the photo section, decide if there are some slides that everyone wants. Before getting copies or prints made, decide who is paying for what. You can buy machines that will let you scan slides directly onto your computer or you can look for a service in your area that does this for you. The quality of scanning services varies widely so shop around. You often get what you pay for.

Home movies

I recommend that you give movies to someone who has a way to view them, (look around the house for an old projector), and has time to take a look through them and make notes of what is on each reel. From there, select those that you want to save. Copy them onto disks or thumb drives to distribute to all in the family who want copies. Again, decide who pays for what before you commit to getting copies and mailing them.

Photography Equipment

The option that works best for most people is to donate the equipment to a local high school or community photography club. If some of these items are from a professional studio, contact a local photographer and ask for advice on who might want these supplies.

Plants

Regular house plants are best dispersed by asking neighbors or perhaps posting on **Freecycle**, **Next Door** or similar app. If you are dealing with a collection of specialty indoor plants such as African violets, orchids or bonsai for example, look for a community club that specializes in raising these plants. Call your agricultural department county extension agent and ask for a list of local gardening clubs. The clubs often have specialty groups that grow your particular plant and would love to have your collection. A local gardening or plant store may also know of local plant and flower clubs.

Religious Items

If there are religious items no one in the family wants, call the appropriate faith community and ask if they would like them. This might include indoor and outdoor statues, pictures, posters, jewelry, books and holiday decorations and dishes.

Rugs, Carpeting and Carpet Scraps

Area rugs are good donation or resale items if they are clean and in good condition, otherwise throw them out. Smaller pieces of carpeting and carpeting scraps, in good condition are best donated to animal shelter and rescue organizations; call before you haul!

Under limited circumstances rugs, especially bathroom rugs, are accepted by charitable thrift stores if they are in very good condition. Call to see what sizes of rugs and carpets the store has space for. Please wash kitchen and bath rugs prior to donating.

School Memorabilia

Schools from elementary to high school, technical to college are usually thrilled to get items that represent the school's past if the item is unusual or of historic value. Whether it is a collection of photographs, a letter sweater or commemorative paperweight, contact the school to ask if they would like what you have and how to donate the items.

If the school is local, deliver the items personally along with any notes you might have found or some information on the family member to whom the item belonged. If you are donating your father's sweater, it means much more to the school if they know when he attended and graduated, some information about how he came to letter, and a bit more about the rest of his life. For schools far away, contact the alumni office and let them know what you have and where you live. If it is difficult to get the item to the school, perhaps they can inform you of a local alumnus who might be interested in what you have.

Sewing Machines

Sewing machines in good working order are in demand by thrift stores and groups that work with low-income and refugee populations. For newer, fancier machines and sergers call a local sewing machine dealer to see if they sell used machines. A machine that is an antique, such as a treadle, could be sold through an antique dealer or given to a museum; call before you haul.

Sports Equipment

Some cities have second-hand stores that buy and sell used sports equipment; most buy only in-season items. Sometimes local outdoor organizations have equipment swaps. Local sporting goods stores often have this information.

For sports of general interest there is usually a local dealer who sells equipment and supplies whom you can call for resale or donation ideas. Some equipment for sports such as baseball, softball, basketball or hockey can be used by local community youth teams. To find them, call your city or county recreation department. Schools in low income neighborhoods also appreciate newer, general sports equipment in good condition, especially soccer balls.

For motor boats and sail boats see section on CARS; for camping equipment CAMPING section. For specialty sports such as archery, fencing, or field hockey, go online. The web has multiple sites for every sport, large or small, with links to local clubs and online resale bulletin boards. Be creative in your use of terms. For bow and arrows you may search for the terms "archery" or "bow hunt." Each term produces slightly different results.

Here are tips for a few of the more popular sports across the country:

Boating – Motorboats are discussed in CAR section. Canoes and kayaks are may be resold online, through a dealer, or by posting an ad at local retail outlets who have customer BUY/SELL bulletin boards. Don't forget to post a picture. When contacting the retailer, be prepared to tell them as much of the following information as possible: brand, how many it seats, material, age, condition (scrapes, dents), whether or not you have paddles, and if so, how many. Rubber rafts are a bit more difficult. Call a local sporting goods store and ask them for ideas. There may be a rafting club or youth group who could use them. Youth camps are an outside possibility depending on what you have to donate. Don't forget to include life jackets and things like patch kits or touch-up paint that go with the boat. If selling a canoe or kayak, look around to see if you can offer a car roof rack as part of the deal.

Bowling – Call the local bowling alley to see if they accept used bowling balls, bags and shoes. If not, they may be able to put you in touch with a local league who may know of someone looking for the items you have. If you live near the alley, the owner may let you post a flyer advertising what you have. Be sure to include brand of ball, weight, bag and shoes, shoe size and whether items are for a man or woman. Listing colors or providing a picture may also be helpful.

Fishing – Call a local business that sells gear and tackle. They will be able to help you with ideas of groups that may be able to use old poles and other miscellaneous gear. They might also know of someone who resells fishing equipment.

Golf – Contact a local golf supply company, golf course or club to find out if they accept donations or offer resale opportunities. They can also help you find an appraiser if you know or believe the clubs to be of great value. Ask them, too, about resale of shoes, bags, carts, balls and other accessories. There are markets for partial sets of clubs, so call before you throw them out. You can also call your County Recreation department to see if there is a junior golf program to which you can donate items.

Ski equipment – Styles, sizes and safety features change over the years. If skis, boots and bindings are more than five years old, they are not of use anymore. Call a store that specializes in selling this equipment if you need help figuring this out. They will want to know the kind of skis, downhill or cross country, brands of skis and bindings, age, if known, brand and size of boots, and type of poles. It is also helpful to measure the length of the skies. Very old wooden skis are sometimes resold at area antiques stores or retro stores for decorations.

Snowshoes – Newer shoes may be resold through an area sporting goods store that has a resale department. Very old shoes are sometimes sold by local antiques dealers, again as decorations.

Racquets – Whether you have racquets for tennis, squash or other sports, sizes and materials have changed over the years. Check with a store that sells racquets or a local club to find out whether you have an obsolete one. Old tennis balls make good dogs toys. Other, smaller balls that have lost their bounce may be choking hazards if given to larger dogs. Throw them out.

Telephones

Single line telephones may still be used by low-income people or seniors. However, they must be new enough to come with wall jacks. Donations are often taken by local thrift stores and agencies that serve low-income these groups. Old rotary and wired-in touch-tone phones are now obsolete, but can sometimes be used as theater props or sold at "retro" stores.

Mobile phones are useful for domestic violence victims, as they can be programmed to call just 9-1-1 in cases of emergency. Shelters can be found by calling your local police department NON-EMERGENCY number. Not all types of mobile phones can be used for this program. Call the shelter before delivering your phones. Any mobile phone that no longer works can be recycled. Call a local mobile phone store to see if they accept phones for recycling or ask if they can refer you to a community group that does. There are also companies online that will recycle your old phones. Gazelle is one company that may not only buy your old mobile phone but also send you a prepaid shipping label, even for phones they don't buy. Everything is recycled.

Tools

Before donating any tool, check to make sure it is rust-free and in good working condition. Power tools must be operational. Hedge trimmers and similar tools should be sharp. All handles should be in one piece and not being held together with anything like duct tape, glue or nails.

Small hand tools - Hammer, screwdrivers, pliers, in GOOD condition can be used by any number of nonprofit agencies, especially those that own property they must maintain. The agency may also welcome items such as screws and nails, nuts and bolts, miscellaneous hardware items, work gloves, extension and power cords. Small power tools, especially drills and electric screwdrivers will also be helpful. In some areas, Habitat for Humanity operates Restore, a hardware type thrift store. They do NOT accept bags or jars of random nails and screws. Donations must be packages with size and other specifications on the label. Recycle everything else at a metal recycling plant if possible.

Yard tools - From trowels to shovels, and clippers to rakes, all these items make good donations to group homes and community centers that have yards to tend. When calling, ask if they are in need of other items you might have like a lawn mower, snow shovels, weed killer and fertilizer. Community gardening programs, especially those for low-income people always welcome gardening tools, seeds that are not too old, and anything useful for starting seeds indoors. Consider donating any gardening or work gloves you have, too.

Power tools - General power tools, including table saws and circular saws, may also be useful to those organizations mentioned above. Call around and see if community centers or schools that offer woodworking classes can use these and more specialized tools such as routers.

Toys and Games, Puzzles, Game Tables

Toys make good thrift store donations. These along with games and puzzles may also be useful to schools running after school youth programs, drug and alcohol rehabilitation centers, or local senior centers. Before donating these items, MAKE SURE all puzzles are complete, and game pieces and instructions are included. If in doubt, throw it out. For colorful puzzles missing some pieces and random games pieces, play money etc. consider calling someone listed in the Art and Crafts section see if they can use these pieces for craft projects.

Game tables – Whether small, like checker or chess tables, or large like ping pong, foosball or pool tables call local youth and recreation centers, drug and alcohol rehabilitation centers or faith communities that offer youth after-school recreation programs. Be sure to ask whether they can pick up the table or if you need to deliver the item.

Electronic games – Game systems become obsolete very quickly. Call thrift stores, group homes or any other organization you are thinking of donating to see if they will accept your item. They will need to know the make and model of the system, if your donation includes compatible games and what those games are, working controllers and anything else you can tell them about the system. For gaming systems that are extremely old, recycling is your best option.

Handheld electronic games are great donations for resale or for kids in any number of programs. If giving these games to a kids program, please consider including some batteries so the fun can continue on for a while.

Computer games – See COMPUTERS

Trophies and ribbons

Very old trophies may be purchased by antique stores. Some youth sports clubs may like bigger trophies, with the name plaques removed. Otherwise, throw them out. If you want to preserve the memory, take a picture first or make a list of trophies received and what they were for. Some trophies also have removable plates that can be saved if desired.

Videos

Movies, TV shows, sports matches and other programs that are home-recorded from TV or burned onto CDs from your computer are of no use to anyone. Throw them out. Commercial recordings, depending on the type of movie, may be appreciated by adult day care or senior centers, nursing homes, rehabilitation centers, domestic violence or homeless shelters, after-school and summer programs or thrift stores.

For tips on what to do with home videos see PHOTO section in this chapter.

Wigs, Toupees and Hairpieces

There are two primary types of people who can use these items: cancer patients, and amateur actors. If the style of a wig, toupee or hairpiece is modern, and hair quality and condition are excellent, an organization that works with cancer patients may be able to use them. If not, call your local school drama department or community theater group. It should go without saying that any item that smells musty, greasy, bad, or "off" should be discarded.

Yard Chemicals and Fertilizers

Your best bet is to offer these to neighbors or through Freecycle. If you do need to dispose of these items, please call your local health department to find out when and where hazardous waste is accepted.

Yard Equipment and Tools

Many nonprofit organizations, including faith communities that are in owner-occupied, freestanding buildings may be happy to have a newer lawn mower, leaf or snowblower, ladder, or hedge trimmer. Call first to inquire about needs. Ask if the organization can pick up the items or if you need to provide delivery. Be sure everything is in good working order, and if possible include the owner's manual for each power tool along with any extra oil or fuel that may be in the shed or garage. You might also ask about their need for tree clippers, rakes, garbage containers, snow shovels and ice melt/sidewalk salt.

Yarn, Crochet and Knitting Needles

Full skeins of yarn along with crochet hooks or knitting needles can be donated to local groups that make afghans, hats or scarves for charity. These groups include seniors, 4H and Girl Scouts. Some churches make prayer shawls. Don't forget to inquire as to whether they would like other accessories such as row counters, yarn caddies or patterns. Partial skeins, or yarn scraps, can be donated to groups that need art and craft supplies.

Final note

Clearing a home of possessions, large and small, is a daunting task. Remember to take the job in small pieces, one drawer or shelf at a time. There is no right or wrong way to go about the process. The important thing is to keep moving forward. Celebrate each small victory – one closet emptied, two bags of clothes taken to charity – whatever it takes to provide you and those helping you with continuous positive reinforcement. Try to empty some floor space as you go along. Seeing a clear corner can do wonders to boost your spirits and visualize progress.

Be kind to yourself as you go through the process and remember to take breaks and recharge with good food and plenty of water. You can do this! And if needed, bring in a professional organizer to help.

Chapter 3

Dealing with all those papers

Papers stuffed in drawers throughout the house, files in the basement, boxes in the garage and attic. It's enough to give you nightmares! Unsure how to start sorting? Don't know what you MUST keep? This is the chapter for you.

Initial Sort

Similar to the system outlined in Chapter 1, make sorting cards for boxes or other containers. Start with the following categories: BILLS, BUSINESS, PERSONAL, SUBSCRIPTIONS, GARBAGE, DON'T KNOW. See expanded list below to help determine what goes in which pile or box.

First do a quick sort into these major categories. From there you can split up piles among family members or you may want to deal with piles such as "bills" or "business" now and leave the personal pile for another time. Put items into the category that seem the best fit at FIRST glance. Later you may find out what at first glance looked like a credit card bill may only be a solicitation for a new card. That's OK. But for now the key is to do a QUICK sort so everything is in a labeled container.

Here are guidelines for what to put in each pile:

BILLS – anything that needs or might need to be paid, statements for medical services even if they say "not a bill, for information purposes only," stubs from utility bills for the last three months, receipts for medical bills dated within the last 12 months, last monthly statement for all other bills.

BUSINESS – non-medical insurance papers, bank statements, any paperwork related to Social Security, stocks, annuities, retirement accounts etc., titles, deeds, canceled checks, credit cards, business cards. Items to also include are cards for professional services – dentist, podiatrist, yard care, etc.

PERSONAL – all personal letters recent and historic, holiday cards, invitations, birthday and anniversary cards.

SUBSCRIPTIONS – include magazines, paid professional newsletters and journals, unpaid newsletters from clubs and the faith community to which the deceased belonged.

UNSOLICITED MAIL – You know what this is! Double check this pile after the initial sort before throwing out.

MISC/DON'T KNOW – anything that at first glance may or may not be important; membership card for a gym, roadside assistance etc., membership or award certificates, anything that doesn't fit into the above categories at first glance.

If pictures are mixed in with the papers, put them in a separate pile and see the PHOTO section in Chapter 2 on how to begin sorting all those photos!

Next Steps

Once you have done a rough sort and have everything in a pile or box, here are some suggestions for what to do next with items in each category. **Note:** There is a nifty gadget called a security ink roller that can be purchased at The Container Store and online. It has a small rolling head with a jumble of numbers and letters that you can just roll across address labels or account numbers on things like magazines. It will save you lots of money on shredding. It is also good for blocking out labels on boxes that you use for donations and prescription pill bottle labels. I don't recommend this for things like bank statements or paper that is mostly filled with private information.

BILLS

Keep a master list for items in this and other categories. It will help you focus on what needs to be done now and when it comes time to sell the property or vacate the apartment. Keeping service phone numbers on your list will make calling for shut-off of services faster and easier. Cancel services such as such as newspaper or milk delivery right now. Do a "next step" sort into MEDICAL and OTHER.

Then further sort OTHER bills by company owed. You need only save utility payment stubs for the month prior to your relative's death unless there are back payments owed or statements showing a balance owed. In that case, keep all statements back to the last statement showing a payment received. Utility payment stubs from months and years before that can safely be tossed unless there was a home-based family business for which utilities are a full or partial write-off. In that case, numerous years of records must be kept. Please call a professional accountant or tax attorney to verify laws in your state. Seven years of records is most common. Be sure to shred or burn items with personal information such as Social Security numbers if they have been used as account or ID numbers.

Bills for current expenses such as light and power can be paid by the estate once the executor has been given authority to write checks. Be sure that previous months' bills are current as of the month your relative died. Keep a list of services as you pay bills so that you know what will need to be shut off, discontinued or transferred when the property is sold or vacated. If there is any dispute with the utility company, previous month's stubs can help verify that the account was not in arrears. Once you have verified that all bills have been paid and the checks have cleared the bank, the remaining stubs can be thrown away. Be sure to put phone numbers for each utility on your master list. Going through this pile will also alert you to services/accounts that you may not have been aware of and will want to cancel now or in the near future. These can include credit cards, cable TV, internet service, cell phone service, ongoing home cleaning and yard maintenance services.

Note: When cancelling cable TV services, be careful to cancel streaming services such as Netflix and Amazon as well.

Next, sort the MEDICAL pile by provider; then organize these papers by date of SERVICE. This will be important when trying to figure out what bills have been paid, what bills are pending, which bills are covered by the insurance companies and which bills you still owe, for final services to your relative, for non-allowable expenses or additional co-pays. Keep EVERYTHING related to medical expenses, as they might be deductible on taxes owed by the estate. And see the insurance section below. Medical bills often take months to resolve, given the complex billing and reimbursement systems between insurance companies and care providers. Until you are absolutely sure that something like ambulance service has been paid in full between you and the insurance companies, keep EVERY piece of paper regarding that particular service.

Business

Depending on how many papers there are in this category and how complicated this is, you can choose to do one of two things. You can sort out business papers by where each account is held, or sort in general piles – stocks, insurance, financial institutions. Make one more pile for cards from professional service providers.

Remember that a final tax return will have to be filed for the deceased, and allowable deductions for the year they died must have accompanying paperwork. Keep everything in this category until these two questions are answered:

1.   Were taxes filed for the last few years? Sometimes an older person will forget this obligation and you will find that you need to gather financial information for more than the last calendar year.

2.   Is there a home office or personal business for which deductions will be made? If so, contact the accountant who has been keeping these records in past years.

Professional services cards

These items will be a mixed bag but it is a good idea to go through all of them. Besides having business cards for medical service providers, there will usually be cards for non-medical or other professional service providers that the deceased used. Check to see if there are any cards listing upcoming appointments that need to be canceled with the dentist, podiatrist, or hairdresser. Then call and cancel appointments and notify longtime providers, such as a dentist, of the death. Confirm that no bills are outstanding. If there is an appointment calendar, be sure to find it and look ahead to other appointments that may need to be canceled, especially with medical specialists. Some will automatically bill you for appointment no-shows if appointments are not canceled well in advance. Charges can often be canceled if the patient has died, but canceling in advance saves trying to straighten out the billing mess with a third-party medical billing service later. Also see if there are other ongoing services like pest control or weekly yard maintenance that need to be canceled. Business cards are good reminders for people who should be notified of a death and services / subscriptions that should be cancelled.

Financial Institutions

Notify all banks and credit unions where the deceased had accounts, regardless of balance, of the death. Do NOT close out all accounts immediately as there may be outstanding checks or pending online automatic payments yet to be cleared. Let those where your loved one had savings, money market or CDs on account know the name and address of the executor. A 1099-INT for each account will need to be sent at year end or when the certificate comes due to be included with the final tax return.

Find out if there are any accounts on auto pay and make a list of what you need to cancel immediately like health insurance, cable TV or the auto club, and what you need to cancel later like utilities.

Be sure to shred or burn all unused blank checks, deposit and withdrawal slips to prevent identity theft AFTER the account is closed. Until then, keep a few of each to pay final bills and deposit final checks. A certified copy of the death certificate will need to be presented before any account can be closed. There may also be other paperwork needed, such as proof you are the executor. Call the bank before you go to see what is needed.

You will also want to verify whether there is a safe deposit box somewhere. Call the bank to see if one or two keys have been issued for the box. After clearing the contents of the box, these keys must be surrendered to the bank before the box can be officially closed. If the second key is missing, you will be charged a hefty fee for a replacement.

Insurance

Car – Call the company holding the policy after you have decided what to do with the car and the plan has been completed. Cancel this policy only AFTER you have sold or donated the car. If you intend to keep the car, be sure it has been added to your current policy before canceling the old. You will want active insurance on the car as long as you and other family members are using it to run errands while in town or if you are leaving the car in a garage for a few months. Ask the insurance agent if there are any other vehicles on the policy. There may be other items on the policy such as recreational or farm vehicles on which payments are also being made.

Home – Whether you own the property or rent, I advise keeping this insurance until the property is sold or vacated. Even if the deceased was a renter, check to see if they carried contents insurance. There may also be riders for jewelry, guns, musical instruments, art or other valuable items. Cancel that coverage only after you have relocated or disposed of the items.

NOTE: If your relative was renting the property, check to see if any deposits for cleaning, security, keys, pets or last month's rent are due you.

Life – Call the insurance company and let them know of the death. They can instruct you as to who the beneficiary is and how that person goes about claiming the policy funds. A death certificate will need to be provided. Work closely with the estate executor.

Stocks, bonds, annuities, retirement

Find the most recent statement and call the stockbroker listed. Notify him/her of the death and ask for paperwork to be sent to you to transfer the accounts. They usually will require a death certificate for each account. Work closely with the executor on this. It is also important to find out if the broker or the deceased has the original stock certificates. Most often an individual will NOT have the original stock certificate, but some might for a feeling of security. In most cases a reputable accountant, lawyer or financial planner should be consulted to deal with items of these types.

Letters and cards

Recent letters and cards – These are people you may need to call now or write soon to inform them of the death, especially if they live out of town. Make a special pile for condolence cards to the family. Some may contain checks for charitable donations. Others may have accompanied flowers that you will need to acknowledge later.

Family correspondence – These are letters you and other family members have sent over the years.

Couple's letters to each other – There may be some real treasures here; letters during their courtship or correspondence during the war. If need be, include these in the family lottery or round robin as described in Chapter 1. You may also want to put these in a box to deal with at a later time when you and your siblings get back together to finalize some of the estate details.

Subscriptions and newsletters

Sort everything into smaller piles, one issue per pile.

Magazines – If you want to continue receiving any magazine until the subscription runs out, you will need to send each magazine publisher a change of address card. The post office will not automatically forward magazines. Remember that the change of address can take up to six weeks. For now, cut the label off one copy of each magazine, put it in a Ziploc bag and deal with the change of address cards later. After that, dispense with each pile as decided earlier – throw, recycle or yard sale. If you are considering donating magazines, see section on BOOKS in Chapter 2.

Newsletters – subscriptions, some of which are free, should be canceled as soon as possible. Again, sort into piles, and if you want to continue receiving any newsletters at your home, save the labels as per magazines. Don't forget to check email and online accounts to make sure you are not receiving bills for accounts you forgot to close.

Unsolicited mail

To prevent identity theft, which continues growing rapidly (yes, even for the deceased!), destroy all unsolicited, pre-approved credit cards and any enticement "checks" and shred accompanying letters containing personal information.

Throw or recycle remaining items, depending on what your family decided at the beginning of the process. See Chapter 1 for more details.

Misc/Don't Know

This pile might contain auto club cards, library cards, papers from a movie rental service or items which at first glance may be important or could be junk.

Club memberships and cards

Notify groups like the auto club of the death. Before the account is closed, verify that no fees are outstanding. If they are, ask for a final itemized billing to be sent to the executor for payment. For the library and movie rental service, ask whether any materials are currently checked out and owed back. If so, make a note of exactly which items to look for around the house and then ask that the account be listed as closed so that no one else can use it. Upon return of the final items, cancel the account. If there are fines owing, they may be waived if you explain the situation to the librarian or rental service. It is also wise to cancel memberships such as those to warehouse shopping clubs that are said to be non-transferable. This is just extra insurance to cover you.

Chapter 4

Tips for Downsizing

This chapter deals with moving yourself or a relative to a much smaller living place with very limited space such as a small condominium in a senior complex, a studio apartment or a room in an assisted living facility. The previous chapter will help you with ideas on where to donate items you're not taking with you, especially those beyond what usual charity thrift stores accept.

This is also the time to assess the needs for your new lifestyle. Will you really need your china? What about that collection of commemorative plates? Now may be a good time to think about who you would like to have those things. Your daughter may be thrilled to get the family china now, especially since family celebrations are now at her home. A granddaughter may feel quite honored to receive a set of your fancy glasses as a graduation or wedding present. Think about giving each grandchild a piece of jewelry for a holiday or birthday gift – if it is something they will treasure. You will have the pleasure of seeing their smiles, and you will still be around to tell them about the item you have passed on. If no one in the family wants your doll collection or crystal ashtrays, get over it and send them to consignment or a local thrift store. And by all means DO NOT offer them to a friend who is a hoarder just to keep them in "the family". Think of the good that will come from the money made by the charity that runs the thrift store.

Before you move to your new living space, if possible, measure all floor and closet space in the actual unit you will occupy. Note how many built-in cupboards there are in each room. There may not be a coat closet, in which case you should keep a small coat rack if you have one. Otherwise leave room in the bedroom closet for coats and sweaters. If there is no linen closet or cupboard, take this into account when deciding how many sets of sheets and towels to take.

Wall space is also important to measure. Just a few pictures can fill up a living room wall in a small apartment. Depending on lighting, table and counter tops may need to be available for lamps instead of figurines and framed photos.

By far the biggest challenge to downsizing is how much to take with you. Years ago when I moved my grandmother to assisted living, we had a place for everything that was going in her room. The move was quick and easy. I will never forget the angst of a woman moving in just down the hall. She was telling her grandsons to leave the china hutch in the hall. There was no place to put it in her room.

As I walked by and glanced in, I saw furniture piled to the ceiling. The mother and daughter were fighting over whether to take the china hutch away or get rid of half the stuff in the room so the hutch could fit. The grandsons were mad at the thought of reloading the hutch on the elevator and putting it back in the moving truck. And, one said, "What are we supposed to do with all the boxes still on the truck?"

Moving day is stressful enough! Don't let this happen to you. Plan ahead, then plan some more!

Here are some questions to ask regarding each room:

Kitchen

Will any appliances be in the room or apartment?

If laundry service is included, no need to take the laundry basket, clothes drying rack or clothespins. Leave the laundry detergent, fabric softener and dryer sheets behind, too, if you won't be doing laundry anymore. If hook-ups are available, do they accommodate your current appliances? Don't go to the trouble of moving in a gas-powered dryer only to find out there is only an electrical outlet available. Efficiency laundry areas may only have space for stacking apartment-size washer/dryer units.

If there is a stovetop in your new home but no oven, no need to take baking sheets or muffin tins. Some assisted living facilities don't even have a small refrigerator in the room. Know before you go.

Am I going to receive most of my meals in a central dining room?

If the answer is yes, then there will be little need to take items such as a crockpot or lots of pots and pans. Taking into account what appliances you will have, consider what basic needs you want to meet. If you like a glass of juice first thing in the morning, keep a few glasses and a pitcher. Picky about coffee? Take your coffee maker and a coffee cup or two for guests. If popcorn is your favorite snack, by all means take you electric popcorn popper — as long as there is a place to store it and you will use it often! Perhaps popcorn is just a sometimes snack. In that case think about switching to microwave popcorn if your new place has a microwave oven. Or better yet, just buy a bag of pre-popped corn!

If you will be cooking for yourself remember how many you will be serving at any time. Perhaps that set of dishes for 12 is excessive. Give eight-place settings to one of your kids and make sure they get the rest of the set after you are gone. Thinking of keeping the whole set in case everyone comes over for birthday cake? Now is the time to think about having cake and ice cream on paper plates on those special occasions. It is not the dishes that will make a difference, it is the company!

Do you need china, everyday and holiday dishes? One set may be plenty. Take your favorite set, even if it is china. Live out your life eating in luxury! How many small appliances will you use regularly? It only makes sense to take the crockpot if you will use it often. Only used it once in the last five years? Don't move it; you won't miss it. Think about thinning out things such as serving spoons and kitchen knives. Ten of each might be a bit much.

Will there be room for a small kitchen or dining table?

If so, then consider taking a tablecloth or a few placemats to go on the table. If not, and space allows, you might want to take some TV trays in case you have a friend over for a meal or tea. ONE centerpiece is quite enough if you will be taking your kitchen table. If there is only a snack bar, you may be able to take only two chairs or stools with you. Don't break up a dining set. Sell it or give it away, and buy something new.

Be sure to assess wall space too. There may be no room for a kitchen wall clock and a hanging mug rack and a cute picture. Which item is most important?

Bedroom

Will you have a separate bedroom, or will your bed be your primary piece of furniture?

If your bed will be the primary furniture item in the room, make sure the bed you are taking will fit and allow you enough space to get around the room comfortably. This also applies if you will have a private bedroom. Is it really necessary to keep your king, queen or even double bed? Take only sheets that fit the bed you are taking, and just enough pillows for each bed. Remember that you may have storage limitations. Also, think about how many blankets you will really need and pick ONE bedspread for your bed. Don't forget that there is room to store items under the bed. It is a great place to keep off-season clothes or your extra set of sheets and towels.

For those who will be living in a single room or studio apartment, the first thought may be to take a sofa bed or futon for aesthetics and to provide more space during the day. I recommend you think twice about doing this. One reason is your back. Will your old sofa bed or futon give your back the support it needs? A better-looking apartment is not worth continuous nights of uncomfortable sleep and continuous days with an aching back. Do you have the physical strength to pull out and put back the sofa bed each day? Do you want the bother?

How big is the bedroom closet? Is there a coat closet?

For hanging clothes, measure the length of the hanging rod in the new place and put a mark on the rod in your old closet. Play the Trading Game, detailed later in this chapter, until everything fits in the allotted space. This also applies to shelves built in to the closet. Do you need one or more to store hats, gloves, or extra blankets?

Is there room for a large dresser or just a chest of drawers?

Check this out and also assess what other storage is available for clothing. If you have limited storage and need to fit most of your clothes in one chest of drawers, pack your clothes accordingly. Taking a large armoire that has nowhere to be stored will result in your weeding out clothes in your new location. Play the Trading Game, as detailed later in this chapter, before you move anything to your new home.

Moving is difficult. Make sure unpacking goes as smoothly as possible after you arrive. Don't make the mistake of taking a dresser and chest of drawers to find out only one fits in your new room.

What are your lighting needs?

As we age lighting becomes more important. Your new bedroom may have built-in lighting that is adequate for all your needs. On the other hand, you may need to take a strong bedside lamp for reading, safety and convenience. Be sure to figure out if there is room for one or two nightstands and if those you currently own will fit. Maybe a good reading light will have to be mounted on the wall, if allowed. Some facilities have no overhead lighting at all. Double check each room to see if this is the case.

Will you want a TV in your bedroom?

If the answer is yes, make sure to check for hookups in that room. Nothing is more frustrating than moving a TV and finding out there is nowhere to hook it up in the room where you planned to put it. Be sure to measure the area where you plan to put it. There may not be room for the big screen TV you currently own. You may want to buy a smaller unit to put on your dresser or chest of drawers instead. Take this into account when packing bedroom knick-knacks. Do you have a table or TV stand that fits the TV you are taking or plan to purchase? If floor space is at a premium, measure your wall space to see if there is a good place to hang a flat screen TV. Check to see if the facility even allows you to put up a wall-mounted TV.

Bathroom

Your challenge here will most likely be counter space and cabinets available for storage. Towels may have to be stored in another room or utility closet. This goes for personal items such as your scale, hair dryer, or foot massaging machine. Measure the cabinet space, and if necessary mock up the space at home and play the Trading Game. Counter space is important to consider too. Rechargeable items like toothbrushes and razors need space. Bathroom gadgets have a way of multiplying! What do you use frequently? Make note of available plugs and count the outlets. Again, check to see if the facility will allow you to mount a small cabinet or shelf on the wall. Often you will have to buy a rack that sits on the floor with shelves that go over the toilet.

Living Area

This is the hardest area to assess. If at all possible prior to moving, get the exact measurements of the room's floor and wall space.
Is there room for a full size sofa, just a love seat, or is it necessary that room be made for your favorite recliner?

If you are taking a recliner, make sure there is enough space in the room to open it. The less furniture you move, the better. You want room to move around and not feel cramped. Be sure there is space between pieces to move around using a walker. Even though you may not use one now, it pays to plan for the future and possible visitors. Also, you entertainment needs are changing. You may not need seating for many visitors in your new room. Your new residence may well have common areas with plenty of seating for visiting family and friends.

Does the place where you are moving have an activity room or club house?

Can you find games and puzzles there? Are there games that are very important to you? If you like to play Scrabble and chess often, by all means take those items with you. If you like to play bridge often, does your building have a table and chairs somewhere or is there a condo clubhouse available for entertaining your bridge club? If the grandkids like to play Monopoly when they come over, have them bring the game with them. Or take this opportunity to teach them bridge or Scrabble!

In short, what is the primary activity you will be doing in your new space?

Reading, watching TV, sewing, inviting friends over for coffee or drinks? Pick your furniture items keeping this thought at the forefront.
Is there room for a curio or china cabinet?

If there is room for something like this, make sure you play the Trading Game BEFORE you pack anything for the move. Be reasonable about how much will fit. I have seen lots of frustration with families trying to pack three times more into a curio than will fit and then have to repack and take away figurines and dishes. This is quite distressing for everyone!
Are there built-in bookshelves or will you be taking a bookcase? Is there room for a bookcase in any room?

If you are taking one or more bookcases, you need to play the Trading Game BEFORE you pack any books or knick-knacks that you want to display on your bookshelf. Again, be reasonable about how much will fit. Leave a little bit of space for future acquisitions. Consider whether a public library is close by, whether your new complex has its own library and/or whether the place you will be living has weekly van service to a library. If you are a voracious reader, consider buying an electronic book reader instead of keeping lots of books. One advantage to electronic readers is that the type can be made bigger in an instant for easier reading. Do you really want to move shelves to display your entire doll or ceramic owl collection? For that matter do you want to pack and move the collection itself? Perhaps now is the time to consider giving those items to family or friends, or a local thrift store.

Will you be taking your VCR, disk player or stereo system, or computer?

If you answered yes, consider additional space needed to store records, tapes, CDs and movies. Does your new complex have movie night each week? Is there a good classical music station where you are going? Can you subscribe to movies online or check out favorite titles from your local library? Does the TV service at your new residence have streaming music channels? Do you need a special desk for your computer? You might not need to take as much as you think.

What lighting is in the room?

Determine what lighting is in place and how many floor and /or table lamps will be needed. Table lamps will also need side tables so figure out how much space they will take too. Try to visit your new apartment once at night, especially if your eyesight is poor. Rooms that seem to have adequate light during the day can be much darker than anticipated at night.

Outside the Condo or Apartment

Is there a patio, small balcony or deck?

If so, you should measure the space and determine how much outdoor furniture and how many planter boxes or flowerpots will fit. Bringing the gas grill may not be the best idea. Is it even allowed? But having a chair and one large flower pot on the balcony may bring a lot of joy. NOTE: many senior living and care centers will not let you bring anything that you light with matches including candles.

Is there a storage closet, shed or garage that comes with the unit?

If you celebrate Christmas, moving an artificial tree, even a small one, may not be a consideration if it needs to be stored inside your new living space. Consider too, how much space decorations for any holiday and different seasons take up. Is there even room to put lots of holiday decorations up in your new space? Will you be hanging a wreath on your front door for each season?

If you will only have a small storage closet outside your apartment or condo, measure that and trace it out on the floor at home. This can also be done by determining how many plastic storage tubs or crates will fit inside the storage space. What about keeping all your luggage? If you will be traveling, determine the maximum number of pieces you will actually use at one time and donate the rest to charity.

The Trading Game

When you have chosen all of the furniture you are going to move, empty pieces such as the curio cabinet, bookshelf or dresser well in advance of your move. Then play the trading game.

Playing the trading game before you move will help you prioritize which items to move. Is it more important to have a crystal bowl or commemorative plate? Will you be more likely to use a candy dish or glass vase? Unpacking at your new home will also be a breeze if everything you bring has some place to go.

Start with one piece of furniture. Let's take the curio cabinet as an example. Put into the cabinet the items you consider most important to take with you. Once the cabinet is full and only part of the items you want to take are inside, you must start trading. For any other item to be put into the cabinet, one must be taken out. This can be very emotional, even painful, so take your time. You may need a few days to trade items back and forth. This way, once you get to the new location, everything you unpack will have a place to go. Settling in will be so much easier. Ask your nieces, nephews, grandchildren or friends if they would cherish one of your figurines. If they say yes, consider giving your extras to them as a gift for a birthday, special holiday or graduation. Write out something about the object on an index card — why it is special to you and how you came to own it. Ask the parent to store the objects at his/her house until the appropriate time. The recipients will truly cherish the gift, and you will get the joy of seeing them receive it. That also opens the door to telling your family more about that period of your life, and you can relive cherished memories. Don't forget to play the trading game with drawers that are in the cabinet. Not as many placemats, doilies, tablecloths, needlework kits or skeins of yarn fit in those drawers as you think!

More than anything, be realistic about your new living situation. How many things will you need for the next phase of your life? How important is it to hang on to those knick-knacks? Are you really going to keep sewing or doing crafts? Will you truly be riding your bike again?

A note to adult children: Try to include your parent in as many decisions as possible. The more opportunities you give an aging parent to decide what will be moved and what will not, the more empowered he/she will feel during this difficult time. If your parent has chosen to move the curio instead of the extra bookcase, you will be less likely to be blamed when the bookcase is left behind. Having your parent play the trading game also provides a sense of empowerment and provides a reality check for how many things it is realistic to move.

Before finalizing your move, notify all friends, businesses, etc. of your new address. You might even order or print out a set of return labels with the new address. Printing up simple business cards with new address, and phone number if applicable, is also a great idea.

Downsizing can be a freeing experience. It can be a time to simplify your life and divest yourself not only of possessions but responsibilities as well. Passing on dishes and decorations along with the tradition of holiday meals from your home to someone else's helps with letting go.

Packing, moving and unpacking a household, whatever the size, takes a lot of time and effort. It can also be expensive. **Be sure that everything has a purpose AND a place.**

Enjoy the fact you will now have less space to clean, fewer things to dust, fewer places to search for misplaced items and lower, or even no utility bills. Celebrate no longer having to put the garbage out, cooking dinner every night or worrying about repairs. It can be joyful and very liberating! May you be successful in your quest to sort through the past.

Linda Hilton is the owner of Sorting Through, a comprehensive organizing company. She works with clients to clear homes, garages, storage sheds and more. Retired from a career in working with low income and homeless people, she understands the importance of finding the highest and best use for everything people no longer want. Keeping items out of local landfills is also of paramount importance. Her goal is helping clients to let go of unused items so they can have a new life with someone who needs them.